Multicultural Teaching

A guide for the classroom

McGRAW-HILL series for Teachers

Consulting Editor
Peter Taylor
School of Education, Bristol University

Multicultural Teaching
A guide for the classroom

Malcolm Saunders
Bradford College

McGRAW-HILL Book Company (UK) Limited

London · New York · St Louis · San Francisco · Auckland · Bogotá · Guatemala
Hamburg · Johannesburg · Lisbon · Madrid · Mexico · Montreal · New Delhi
Panama · Paris · San Juan · São Paulo · Singapore · Sydney · Tokyo · Toronto

Published by
McGRAW-HILL Book Company (UK) Limited
MAIDENHEAD · BERKSHIRE · ENGLAND

British Library Cataloguing in Publication Data

Saunders, Malcolm
    Multicultural teaching: a guide for the
    classroom.—(McGraw-Hill series for
    teachers)
    1. Children of immigrants—Education—
    Great Britain
    I. Title
    371.97   LC3747.G7
    ISBN 0–07–084133–0

Library of Congress Cataloging in Publication Data

Saunders, Malcolm.
    Multicultural teaching.
    (McGraw-Hill series for teachers)
    Bibliography: p.
    Includes index.
    1. Intercultural education—Great Britain—Curricula. 2. English language—
    Study and teaching—Great Britain. 3. Stereotype (Psychology)
    I. Title. II. Series.
    LC1099.S28   371.97   81–20729
    ISBN 0–07–084133–0   AACR2
12345 LT 85432

Printed and bound in Great Britain by
Latimer Trend & Company Ltd, Plymouth

To Joan

Contents

Chapter 4   Language teaching   44
'What can the general teacher do to help the language development of children from the ethnic minorities?'
'What language medium should be used to teach curriculum content to children whose first language is not English?'
'What are the implications of living in a linguistically diverse society for the language teaching of children from the majority ethnic group?'

**Chapter 5   Identity, self-concepts, minority group children   72
and the teacher**
'Why are the concepts of identity and self-concept important for teachers?'
'What is the particular significance of these concepts for multicultural education?'
'What are currently important views on the implications of identity and self-concept for teachers?'

CONTENTS

Preface

Recognizing the multicultural characteristics of the school population as well as of society as a whole, this book is concerned with the implications of this fact for the education of children of indigenous families as well as for children of families of recent settlement.

Accepting the allegations of racism in the teaching profession—whether overt or concealed, deliberate or unwitting—teachers should be helped to recognize racism in themselves and others and to understand the effects of racism on people of other ethnic groups. I have attempted to do that here.

As well as its sensitizing function, this book is designed to help teachers systematically to construct, implement and evaluate multicultural curricula based on an explicit rationale.

While specific teaching techniques are discussed where appropriate, this book deals also with broad guidelines that apply to teaching and learning processes at all levels from first schools through to upper schools and further education.

I acknowledge the help I have received from many quarters in clarifying my ideas on multicultural teaching, not least from colleagues at Bradford College. Miss Kay Baxter of McGraw-Hill has made the preparation of the text for publication much less onerous than it would otherwise have been, for this I am grateful. I thank Professor David Pratt of Queen's University, Ontario, for allowing me to adapt his word list for use in a British context and the help of Mr David Robinson and his pupils and various groups of students in doing this. Finally, I recognize my debt to my wife Joan for the support which has enabled me to apply myself to this task.

Malcolm Saunders
August 1981

1
Introduction: value position and summary of the text

'Do we need to take account of the ethnic backgrounds of pupils in designing, teaching and evaluating the curriculum?'

1.1 Introduction

One of the major characteristics of Britain at the present time is its cultural diversity. Over the last 30 years numbers of people of South Asian and Caribbean origins have added to the displaced Europeans who escaped to this country from Hitler's genocidal attacks and from Russian colonization. They joined the Irish, the Jews and many other groups who came to Britain in earlier periods.

The record of the British in receiving people from other cultures is mixed and includes many discreditable episodes of discrimination and exploitation. For example, some 800 years ago, in the shadow of York Minster, many Jews were burnt alive. Whatever the ostensible reason for their deaths, they represented a minority ethnic group who were subjected to the ultimate penalty for their ethnicity. This event illustrates the centrism which is still a major source of concern.

The tendency to centration is exemplified by the assumedly mythical Englishman who, on entering another country, insisted that he should be allowed to pass through the entrance designated for the native population, rather than that labelled 'Aliens'. Piaget's work suggests that decentration, perceiving a problem from a perspective other than one's own, becomes possible at six or seven years of age, yet ethnocentrism, that is centrism focused on a particular ethnic group, can persist into adulthood and can colour all our social perceptions. Centrism can descend into racism when we claim superiority over other groups who are physically different from us and act on that assumption.

1.2 Ethnocentrism and education

The relevance of ethnocentrism to education is that it can influence both the teacher and the pupils. Preiswerk (1980) has identified six ways in which the learning of history, for example, can be distorted and each of these ways is either caused or exacerbated by ethnocentrism. The first of

1

these arises through ambiguity in the definition of terms, which can lead to distortions; difficulties arise because terms such as 'culture', 'civilization' and 'race' tend to be given meaning only through indirect references to situations which are frequently coloured by ethnically oriented perceptions. The imprecision is often associated with assertions which imply that many people are still part of 'nature' and only a few have evolved to a higher stage where their lives are not determined by natural forces. It is assumed that 'civilization' is the highest form of human goal and this is based on such Graeco–European ideals as those embodied in democratic government, fine art and industry, and made available to successive generations through written historical records. Total allegiance to our value system is implicit: the superiority of the united nuclear family and of the nation is unchallenged, as is the desirability of a strong government guaranteeing law and order based on a democracy through a parliamentary political system. Approval of European expansionism is implicit in explanations of the benefits to be gained by converting the heathen to the Christian faith; through the advantages of technology; by describing the privations suffered by white explorers in the face of mosquitoes, swamps and inhospitable natives, and by reference to a 'right' to occupy a country with unexploited natural resources. Many of these perceptions arise from a cultural arrogance which is either normative, in the sense that the goals of other societies are evaluated by the use of ethnocentric concepts such as 'progress', 'modernization' and 'westernization'; or concepts are transferred descriptively, as in the cases of such concepts as 'time', 'space', 'work' and 'family'. Not only can such concepts be misapplied through transfer across cultures, as we see when we examine the work of Kline (1979) on the use of psychometric tests across cultures, they can also be distorted by inappropriate transfer across time. This can occur when concepts such as 'state' or 'nationalism' are applied to ancient civilizations, and when past phases of our own nation are compared with the present stage of others.

Countless illustrations can be quoted for each of the comments made here. For example, Gordon Rattray Taylor produced a book to supplement the *British Genius Exhibition* in 1977. In a remarkably, if understandably, jingoistic display we are told that for generations the 'British people have contributed more than a fair share to the advance of human civilisation' and 'Not only did we start the Industrial Revolution two hundred years ago, pulling ourselves up by our bootstraps and the world after us, but we have maintained that impetus right up to the present'. No mention is made here of any international consensus on where we should be heading; nor is there note of our contribution to the

2

exploitation of other nations and of slavery as an example of this; but we are told, in one sentence, that 'Samuel Plimsoll campaigned against the over-loading of ships, as Wilberforce had campaigned against slavery before him.' In that book we have an expression of the view that progress consists of technological change and that the exploitation of others is justified if it is designed to assist our progress in those terms. Sir Kenneth Clark, in his highly acclaimed series on BBC television called *Civilisation*, by careful selection of his examples, gives the impression that Greek civilization, from which our own has taken root, was of a higher order than that of the Negro. He persuades us to support this conclusion by asserting that the former inspired the beauty of Apollo, while the latter produced only a mask illustrative of fear and darkness. The qualities of thought and feeling of the Greeks and, by implication, ourselves, have contributed to the pursuit of reason, justice and physical beauty, while the 'primitive' imagined a world that was ugly and evil and which was ready to inflict punishment for the least infringement of any insignificant taboo. In this case not only has Sir Kenneth Clark asserted the supremacy of a particular set of human qualities above others as if they were universally accepted absolutes, by his selection of examples he makes *us* appear to possess these and *them* to be devoid of these attributes. By our stipulative definition, this is racist.

Another cause of the injustices that have been and still are perpetrated against ethnic minority groups in Britain is our readiness to resort to negative stereotyping, since this reduces individuals with a few characteristics in common to a mass that is regarded as homogeneous in many respects. Negative stereotyping asserts that the common characteristics of the group are inferior and when they are associated with supposedly racial characteristics we imply that the attributes are genetically determined and cannot be changed regardless of the alterations that may be made to the circumstances in which those people live. The interim report of the Rampton Committee (DES, 1981) asserts that such racist tendencies are displayed by some teachers.

The persistence with which members of the dominant group cling to racial stereotypes can be demonstrated if we recognize the characteristics of, say, Shakespeare's Othello as typifying all Negroes. Another example can be seen in *Fiction for the Working Man* by Louis James (1973). In this survey, James comments on a fictional story of gipsies called *Gideon Giles*, written by Thomas Miller in 1841. James subscribes, maybe inadvertently, to a racist view of gipsies by perpetuating the partial description of them as 'dirty vagrants', thus ignoring both the favourable qualities of those who are still itinerant and the fact that many descendants of gipsies now live in permanent homes.

3

Biased perceptions held by dominant group members of the ethnic minorities lead to discriminatory behaviour against those minorities. If *they* are different from *us*, then we are justified in treating them in less favourable ways. The implications of this conclusion for teachers are twofold: not only can we treat children from the ethnic minorities differently and unfavourably, it is also reasonable that majority group children develop similar perceptions to our own, thus perpetuating the distortions. THIS BOOK IS WRITTEN ON THE ASSUMPTION THAT BOTH THESE PREMISES ARE INSUPPORTABLE.

1.3 Ethnic identity

There are always at least two parties to a social exchange and the behaviour of each party is usually partly initiatory and partly responsive. In a social interaction three basic responses may be induced in a minority group. In the first place they may be so devastated by the discrimination to which they are subjected that they withdraw as far as possible from asserting themselves in the interchange, physically and psychologically, to the extent where they establish ghettos, as in the case of many Jews. Or they may try to lose their ethnic identities and become assimilated into the dominant group. Alternatively, as in the case of some black Americans and to a lesser extent black Britons, they may overcompensate and become belligerently assertive.

The importance of allowing a minority to retain and develop its ethnic identity, even in the cases of those who appear initially to relinquish it in favour of added social mobility, is becoming clearer. The American sociologist Gans (1979) has identified the concept of 'symbolic ethnicity' from an academic perspective and a literary example of this search for identity is described by Arnold Wesker (1980) in a collection of short stories titled *Love Letters on Blue Paper*, he writes:

> The religious roots of Mrs Newman's youth fiercely returned and her daughter recognized that in her mother's refusal to eat unkosher meat, in her dabbling with barely remembered prayers before Sabbath candles were revealed racist not political prejudices; and Marcia wondered, would she too grow into a Jewishness she had not been trained to but only knew of and felt.

In Wesker's graphic description we find embedded the second major assumption on which this book is based. AT SOME POINT IN LIFE MANY HAVE A NEED TO IDENTIFY WITH AND TO EXPRESS THEIR CULTURAL ROOTS, AND THIS CAN BE PREPARED FOR IN CHILDHOOD.

1.4 Aims

The major aims of this book arise from the assertion of a belief in the fundamental importance of non-discriminatory behaviour from the dominant group members as a whole and from teachers in particular. The aims are as follows:

> Teachers should be alerted to recognize overt and covert racism and to an understanding of the psychological processes that may be involved, and their possible effects on pupils.
>
> Teachers should be introduced to particular curriculum strategies and techniques that are currently regarded as good practice in motivating pupils from ethnic minority families to learn in a way that will assist educational progress without severing contact with their cultural roots.
>
> Teachers should prepare pupils from all cultural groups to live in a culturally diverse society.

1.5 Levels of specificity

One of the dilemmas which accompanies research and thinking about the ethnic minorities in Britain is the level of specificity which is appropriate for the purpose of the examination. Is it acceptable and useful for teachers to talk, for instance, of West Indians as a homogeneous group, or should the various islands of the Caribbean be considered as representing a more acceptable level of cultural homogeneity?

Two sides of the debate are illustrated in the book *Minority Families in Britain* edited by Dr Verity Saifullah Khan. In this book Dr Khan argues that the categories used by society at large are both inadequate in reflecting the diversity of populations and in corresponding to the classifications that the people impose on themselves. To use my own example, from the host population: the Welsh are regarded by 'outsiders' as a culturally homogeneous group, but among themselves they clearly identify North Walians and South Walians, and Welsh speakers from non-Welsh speakers. Dr Khan suggests that to use general labels such as 'West Indians', 'Asians' and 'Cypriots' may be expedient, but they represent popular misconceptions which are lacking in precision. On the other hand, Catherine Ballard, in the same volume, makes the claim that whatever the variations between Indian, Pakistani and Bangladeshi communities in Britain, between East African Asians and South Asians settled in various British cities, the similarities among them outweigh the differences when compared with the indigenous British culture. This belief is supported by Cynthia Enloe (1980) in her book *Ethnic Soldiers*, in which she extracts certain common principles in the deployment of ethnic groupings in armies across the world.

For most purposes it is the latter view to which I shall subscribe in this volume. I do so for three main reasons, the first is that the most important contribution the teacher can make to multicultural education is not so much the application of detailed knowledge of each variation of culture and sub-culture, but rather the development of appropriate and humane dispositions and values that influence his actions; these can signal acceptance or rejection of his pupils. Such a value base can lead to teaching responses to children from minority cultural groups either as individuals or as members of a group, as the context of the teaching requires.

Second, it is unrealistic to expect comprehensive, encyclopaedic knowledge from the teacher, but it is realistic to require the teacher to have access to sources of relevant and detailed information of the cultures represented in his class when such information is necessary for specific purposes, and that he should use these sources.

Experience also suggests that when the teacher requires detailed information concerning a child it is usually at the level of the individual and his family that this is required, rather than at the level of his cultural group, since significant variations can be found in values and life styles at the level of the family.

1.6   Structure of the book

In writing this book I see my function as that of a teacher–writer with the task of bringing to the attention of general teachers a flavour of the important issues and opinions in multicultural education at the present time, and to do this by bringing together a selection of the more pertinent best practices and research results, within a comprehensive curriculum framework. Some indications will also be given for continuing study by the teacher. My intended readership is not the specialist teacher, although reading this book may well result in the specialist altering the balance of his curriculum.

The essential purpose of the next chapter is to set the scene for the rest of the book. Without a framework within which to operate, or in the absence of criteria to guide the selection of content, in any context where there is a plethora of material which exceeds what can be considered within the given limits of space and time, the decision to include or exclude material becomes a matter of whim and fancy. This function of a theory or a rationale provides a systematic way not only of selecting content, but of balancing the emphasis between one item of content and another. And this is as relevant in teaching a multicultural curriculum as in writing a book about it.

An effective curriculum framework can serve an instrumental function in the classroom where it can provide a source for generating new ideas for practice. Omissions and discontinuities between theory and practice can cause the teacher to question his professional performance and future plans. There is also the possibility that, as in all creative work, when familiar concepts are brought together in unfamiliar ways new ideas can be generated.

A carefully constructed framework for the practice of teaching can also serve to justify practice. It is, as it were, like looking down a telescope: to look down the theory/practice telescope from theory to practice can help generate ideas for implementation; to look from practice to theory can result in a justification for what we do as teachers.

The theoretical framework that is described here can also have analytic and evaluative functions. In outlining a curriculum framework for multicultural education I shall be attempting to create a link between views of man and society and to point to the implications of these for classroom practice. This will assist you in establishing appropriate criteria for the analysis and evaluation of your role as a teacher in terms that are consistent with what you do and what you value.

In the next chapter the sources from which criteria can be derived for the selection of goals and objectives for education will be discussed and the relevance and implications of each of these for multicultural education will be considered. I shall argue that to define the purposes of education within the present text requires a definition of the kind of society we seek. From a description of the preferred model of society we shall consider the models of education which will aid the achievement of that kind of society. When we have established a structure for multicultural education we shall then end with an examination of the implications of that model for the planned and guided activities of the classroom and for the organization of the school.

1.7 How to use this book

Most publishers complain that teachers read few books about teaching, unless the books are prescribed reading on award-bearing courses; authors have also been known to express similar sentiments. In an attempt to make books more attractive to teachers, writers have been encouraged in recent years to adopt more informal styles of writing and

7

presentation and to fill their texts with ideas that can be translated instantly into classroom practice. The first of these directions is unquestionably desirable in my view, but the second is a matter calling for the exercise of a great measure of judgement.

In addressing the second issue this book is intended not simply to help the teacher fill his pupils' time, but to engage them in experiences that will achieve certain desirable ends. A host of gimmicks come to mind as suitably eye catching and interest provoking to fulfil the more superficial criterion, but unless purposes are carefully worked through and stated with clarity, we may not like our destination when we get to it. It is in my view vital for the professional teacher to be clear in his own mind where he wishes to go, and only then to select those educational experiences that are most likely to help his pupils to arrive at those destinations.

For this reason I regard the next chapter as essential reading if you wish to make the most of this book. By all means dip into the other chapters if that is what you wish to do, but I suggest you read Chapter 2 now and if you already have a model of multicultural education in mind critically compare the one presented here with your own. If you are new to the field I hope the model in Chapter 2 helps you to construct a model of your own.

Now please turn to Chapter 2.

2
A model for a multicultural curriculum

'What are the purposes of education in a culturally diverse society?'

'How can the school curriculum reflect what we value about people and society?'

2.1 Introduction: the bases of curriculum development

Curriculum development in Britain has traditionally arisen from three sources, these are the perceived needs of children and young people, the requirements of society, and the logic of knowledge. In infant and junior, first and middle schools the ostensible focus for the curriculum has largely been the satisfaction of the perceived needs of the child. If this focus persists in a culturally diverse society an ethnocentric curriculum may be the result.

It is possible to argue that, in order to encourage the fullest development of the individual child, it is necessary to aid his complete integration into the dominant culture. It is only in this way that a child, whatever the culture of his home, will fully acquire the social skills that are necessary for upward social mobility. Also, because the British examination system is firmly rooted within a specific cultural tradition, it can be argued that it favours pupils who conform to the accepted body of knowledge and skills of that culture. But for the school to decide to optimize the development of the child according to its own culture-based definition of success may conflict with the aspirations of the ethnic minority to which the child belongs.

The problem which I have just outlined and which will be developed throughout this book is not simply one of contrasting ethnicity, it can also be perceived in any situation where the culture of the school clashes with that of the home. However, it does appear in heightened form when the education of children from minority ethnic groups is examined. A particular form of the problem is examined in a recent book by Maureen Stone called *The Education of the Black Child in Britain*. As a person who was born and brought up in Barbados, the author argues strongly that the ethnic backgrounds of school children should be disregarded in favour of potential examination successes; she also dismisses the motivational influences of their self-concepts. Yet other writers have emphasized the polar opposite of this argument by stressing the preservation of identity as a vital component of education (see Verma and Bagley, 1975; Khan, 1979).

In this chapter it is my intention to develop a rationale for a curriculum that will respond to the cultural variety that characterizes not just Britain, but every other country where migration is a familiar phenomenon at the present time. The proposed rationale will do violence neither to the needs of children nor to the expectations of the ethnic groups from which they come.

First I shall examine briefly the general aims of education. I shall unravel some of the influences of cultural variations on these general aims, as well as outline the principal consequences of cultural diversity for the achievement of these aims.

I shall begin by considering the twin social aims of equality and freedom; then I shall describe the principal social models of cultural diversity, from which a preferred model will be selected that will form the framework for the remainder of the book. Against this background, some models of education will be examined for their compatibility with the selected model of society and, finally, the stipulated model of education will be considered for its specific influences on the curriculum.

2.2 Criteria for curriculum development

Decisions on what should be the aims of education and what should be taught in schools are largely moral and political decisions, guided in part by the pursuit of equality and freedom. A democratic social system is energized by the tensions that are created by these twin goals. This is a view that has been explored by Mary Warnock (1977). In her discussion she also specifies that children 'must be taught what will enable them to work' as well as 'what will employ and expand their imaginative powers'. To attain this bifocal target there must be a consideration of the life that pupils will be enabled to lead after leaving school.

Finding a job and developing the imagination are, however, not ends in themselves, they are instruments for the achievement of equality and freedom. To work is to achieve a measure of control over one's life and to imagine is to create in the mind alternative views of the future: of what is as well as what might be.

There are three sources from which criteria can be derived for the selection of objectives and goals for education, for the choice of teaching methods and for the evaluation of the curriculum, these are as follows:

Epistemology, or the language and logic of knowledge.

The perceived needs of children, derived from our present understanding of how children should develop if they are to become the
kinds of adults we would wish.

The requirements of society, if it is either to be perpetuated more or
less in its present state, or become a different kind of society.

The epistemology of knowledge is culturally invariant. Wherever one
lives, whatever the culture in which one is reared, the structure of the
traditional subjects will not vary and the concepts that are used can be
transmitted across cultures. As was demonstrated in the former British
grammar schools, no concessions need, or even can, be made in a
curriculum based on the language and logic of knowledge to accommodate the variety of backgrounds of children. The pace of the teaching
may be adjusted to suit the rate of learning of the pupils, but the content
of what is taught lies outside these adaptations. Lack of educational
progress in a pupil is explained not in terms of any faults in the
curriculum, but by reference to deficits in the child or his background.
This perspective on the curriculum is discussed by Hirst and Peters
(1970).

A distinctively different view of the source of the curriculum arises
from arguments within the sociology of knowledge. Central to these is
the belief that it is the social context rather than any alleged intrinsic
structure of the subject that determines what is relevant for the
curriculum. The social context determines not just the aims of education, but the content of the curriculum as well as the power structure of
the school. This view is elaborated in Young (1971).

The work of A. S. Neill (1960) was based on a wish to meet the needs
of children not so much in the course of education but as its essential
function. At Summerhill he established a demonstration of how a school
might respond to the needs of children to the fullest extent that remained
consonant with the demands of communal living. The work of such
authorities as John Bowlby and Kellmer Pringle in Britain has tried to
specify what these needs are, and the humanist psychologists, e.g.,
Maslow, Combs and Rogers in America have also contributed to the
debate.

These three perspectives are rarely found in total in any one school,
they are more frequently found as tendencies, but each of them carries
assumptions about the kind of society we seek.

Crucial to our task of defining the purpose of education for social
diversity is the need for a clear, though not necessarily detailed, picture
of the kind of society to which we aspire. No matter what aims we may

11

derive from epistemology and no matter what the potential of individual pupils whom we try to educate and the stages through which they develop, as potential citizens our pupils must live within society as it exists and contribute to its development. It is to these issues that we now move.

2.3 Models of social accommodation: concepts from immigration theory

When people are either forcibly or voluntarily removed from familiar surroundings and begin to live elsewhere a process of adaptation begins that influences both those who are removed and the community that receives them. The concepts 'assimilation', 'segregation' and 'integration' have been used in immigration theory to describe the processes which are involved. Where individuals or groups become 'assimilated' they are absorbed into the majority culture so that differences between the groups disappear and they become part of a relatively homogeneous larger group. There is a good deal of support from Weinberg (1977), Platera (1973) and others for the view that assimilation implies that the minority culture does not merit being preserved and its loss is not to be regretted. The process of 'segregation' involves the setting up of culturally discrete communities, each one with a range of supporting institutions. Examples of the process of segregation can be found in a number of societies where minority groups seek to establish and preserve their uniqueness through isolation from the majority groups of that society, or in situations where the dominant group forcibly segregates minorities. Jewish communities all over the world exemplify the former; black communities in many countries exemplify the latter.

When cultures become integrated the various cultural groups reach an accommodation that neither destroys their cultural integrity nor separates them to the point where contact is lost. It results in a relationship between the groups that is based on cultural reciprocity. Every group is, ideally, encouraged to develop its own cultural characteristics in public so that they can be shared with others.

MODELS OF SOCIETY
The social processes that have been mentioned can lead to three distinct types of society, they are the 'melting pot', the 'cultural pluralist' and the 'multicultural'.

The terms 'cultural pluralist' and 'multicultural' are not entirely satisfactory since they are frequently used in the literature to denote a general concept of diversity. Since there is only limited agreement on the definitions of terms in immigration theory, in this text I shall write on the basis of stipulative definitions. Here the terms will be used to refer to specific models of society.

In the 'melting pot' model the principal intention is to merge all groups to the point where their traditional characteristics are lost and a blend emerges that is unique to the new society. Only enough support is offered to make alienation tolerable for the newly arrived. The broad culture in the form of, say, diet and eating habits, and religious practices, may be ignored, but enough language support may be provided to enable the recently removed to 'get by'. This model is typical of the situations that were found in the early years of the settlement of the United States and in the settlement of Australia.

'Cultural pluralism', on the other hand, encourages immigrants to retain their own cultures in parallel with those of the host community. This has been expressed as 'unity in diversity'. In such a segmented society the immigrants at worst run the risk of establishing ghettos and at best they gain freedom for separate development. An extreme form of such accommodation may be recognized in the situations of many Jewish communities in Britain in the first half of the present century.

'Multiculturalism' permits the retention of existing values and modes of behaviour, yet there is a recognition of the contribution that each culture can offer the others to their mutual enrichment and benefit. The positive interaction of people of all cultures is sought so that their beliefs and customs become part of the common currency of society as a whole. Through this reciprocal process greater tolerance of unfamiliar views and practices will emerge and the existing norms of both dominant and minority group cultures will be healthily challenged.

A culinary analogy may emphasize the differences between the models described here. In the melting pot it is assumed that by pitching all cultures into a common 'pot' a unique flavour will emerge. This will be unlike the original ingredients, although created from them.

The cultural pluralist model resembles a salad: washed but not tossed. Each ingredient forms part of the salad, but only the garlic superimposes its flavour on the other ingredients.

The multicultural model also finds an analogy in a salad, but this one is well and truly tossed in oil. Each ingredient remains recognizable within the salad, but each very subtly contributes its own flavour to the overall ambience; the dominant flavours are muted, but no flavour is lost.

One of the criticisms that may be levelled at the discussions of the models of society and of the analogies is that they provide a static view of society. The reality of any society is that there is a constant process of interaction such as those between the forces in a social class model of society, or by the motivation of powerful individuals such as Martin Luther King in the United States or Indira Gandhi in India.

Several models of social adjustment are described in the literature which take account of the dynamics of the process. Patterson (1971), in her review of absorption theory, identified 'accommodation' as an early and temporary phase of relations between a host population and immigrant groups, which may persist for the first 5 or 10 years of settlement. A minimum level of interaction and mutual adaptation may exist in spheres of life such as work or education or politics. But in more intimate areas such as marriage and neighbourhood life, cultural differences may continue. Alternatively, in certain jobs a working gang may consist entirely of workers of a particular ethnic group, but their lives outside work may be moving towards assimilation in, say, religious observance or leisure pursuits.

In Britain at the present time there is no consensus on the model of society which is to be favoured generally and which can be used by teachers in developing appropriate curricula. This lack of singular purpose is missing not just in the white British, it is also absent from the ethnic minorities themselves. For example, Avtar Brah (1978), in a study of Asian youth in Southall, concluded that those who are either born in Britain or who have lived here for a considerable time are not alien to the 'British way of life' and, if middle class, 'see a continuity' between their own status and that of the British middle class. This conclusion contrasts with the earlier one of Foner (1975); she claimed that, in a study of Jamaicans in Britain, whatever their educational or occupational status, they tended to be regarded simply as blacks and therefore felt alienated from the dominant group.

Much of the evidence that is available to inform us of the broad aspirations of young members of the ethnic minorities in Britain is either anecdotal or polemic. Some studies have, however, been conducted which were concerned with sampling specific aspirations. Townsend (1971), as part of a larger study, sought the vocational aspirations of immigrant pupils; and Brown (1970), Hiro (1971) and Thompson (1974) included the marital wishes of their respondents in their studies. Taylor (1976), in an empirical 'full-length account of the younger generation' of Asian youths in Newcastle upon Tyne found that his respondents aspired to move out of the 'twilight' areas of the city where they lived with their parents, into those areas of the city where they could live alongside other ethnic groups described as 'long-established tenants of whole houses and flats'. They wished to live in areas where neighbours would be respectable and friendly, but not intrusive. In such a community they felt they would be accepted as individuals and allowed to live their own lives. Taylor concluded that the youths he had studied wished to live away from other Asians, and this is supported by my own research in Bradford in 1973, as well as in subsequent conversations. In contrast, Brah (1978) found in her research that despite objecting to the gossiping and curiosity of their elders, her respondents valued the security which they afforded. These conflicting views illustrate the caution that must be exercised in generalizing from research into the opinions of specific groups. For many purposes it is clear that individual hopes and intentions are necessary. These, although crucial for success-ful teaching, are only one group of the variables that determine the direction and extent of the cultural absorption that may be sought.

The assumptions that have guided and informed the argument up to this point are that the decisions made for the current education of specific children and groups of children demand a sensitivity and responsiveness to the wishes not only of the dominant groups in Britain, but also to those of the minorities. Also, while some decisions can safely be made in response to the views of representatives of minority groups, other decisions must recognize the views of individuals.

The problems presented by the longer-term accommodation of ethnic minorities, whatever form they may take, are peripheral to the urgent resolution of more immediate curriculum decisions. But to choose between these models of society poses a dilemma for the teacher and for the education administrator. The melting pot model underestimates the view that education can not only contribute to social change, it can also perpetuate disadvantage. The alternatives to this model are pluralism with its emphasis on diversity and multiculturalism which requires reciprocal relationships. The decisions to seek either type of society can affect not only the development of rational curricula for schools, but also future recruitment into the profession as well as the professional preparation of teachers.

Ideally, since Britain at the present time is in a state of social and political ambiguity it is, arguably, desirable to aim for mutual accom-modation within a multicultural model as this permits the retention of contact by minority group members with their cultural roots, while allowing them to benefit from the indigenous culture. For the in-digenous population contacts are also afforded through which ex-changes can be negotiated. The alternatives of assimilation through the melting pot and segregation through the pluralist models can lead to the dissolution of contact with one or other cultural pool for all ethnic groups, and this may restrict future possibilities for cultural growth.

15

A multicultural model of society encourages reciprocal contact between ethnic groups.

2.4   Models of education for a multicultural society

It is not easy to identify discrete models of education as responses to cultural diversity in Britain, but Weinberg (1977) has described three models that can be identified in the United States:

> The human relations model
> The inter-racial model
> The human rights model

In the human relations approach there is an assumption that people are basically tolerant of other ethnic groups. In those situations where interpersonal conflicts are found they are believed to arise from a failure of individual perceptions. Since it is assumed that faulty perceptions may be corrected, the appeal of this model is that wrongs can be corrected by providing more information about the minority groups. Education can provide information leading to changes of attitudes, hence education is an effective antidote to prejudice.

Inter-racial education recognizes the prejudice that exists at group level against certain ethnic minorities. For instance, the discrimination against Negroes and American Indians in the United States is much more enduring than can be explained simply on the basis of differences in religion, or language, or national origin. But while the ethnic achievements of the minority groups may be celebrated as special events in schools, the approach is essentially defensive as children are not taught to consider the possibility of a society in which colour is not a disadvantage.

The human rights model fits some current practices in America. Group differences are presented as positive attributes of equal worth. The crucial characteristic of this model is that the members of the ethnic groups have a legal and moral right to choose the extent to which they preserve their cultural uniqueness as opposed to receiving cultural preservation as a concession from the dominant group.

Each of these models of education is compatible with either a pluralist or a multicultural model of society. However, the ideal community to which this chapter is committed is one in which racial and cultural tolerance is a salient factor; in which minority groups will have sufficiently strong feelings of identity not to be intimidated by the proximity of other cultures; and within which the greatest possible freedom for self-determination is preserved. The human rights model of education is regarded as consonant with this ideal, as well as being in harmony with the spirit of the so-called 'progressive' movement in British education.

2.5 Accommodation problems: implications for the planned curriculum

Many curriculum programmes have been developed for use in schools with an ethnically mixed pupil population and many of these will be referred to and described at relevant points in this book. Some of these, for example the Schools Council programmes SCOPE (1968–1973) and CONCEPT 7–9 (1972), were developed principally for the teaching of language skills. Other texts have also been published which examine issues related to language teaching. A good example of one of these is Edwards (1979) who makes a valuable contribution to our understanding of some of the language difficulties experienced by pupils of West Indian origin in British schools. Another area of multicultural education which has been better served than most is religious education. Several texts are available on this subject, for example, the Schools Council Working Paper 36 (1971) and Hill (1976).

But despite the material that is generally available there is still a reluctance in many schools to recognize the fact of ethnic diversity in Britain. Even when this fact is acknowledged there is frequently no agreement on the criteria that should be used in developing or adapting relevant curricula. In yet other schools concessions are made, but only with respect to the language development of the minority group children and to religious studies syllabuses.

The intention of the discussion up to this point has been to allow us to arrive at some conclusions regarding the extent to which traditional curricula meet the demands of multicultural/human rights education. This will lead us to the identification of areas of the curriculum where new responses should be made and to a rationale on which the decisions can be based.

Mutual social accommodation based on multiculturalism is espoused here as one of the major directions in which we wish to see society moving. We also accept the human rights model as an appropriate outline for an education process model for achieving these aims. The teacher and the curriculum developer must then seek to translate these theoretical models into a practicable programme. What we are now committed to, from the development of this argument, is the creation of a balanced ethos in which cultural traditions are shared and in which the development of individuals from both majority and minority groups is maximized. In the final part of this chapter I shall suggest the implications of these intentions for the curriculum.

To simplify the discussion, let us assume that a situation exists in which there is only one majority and one minority group. In this context the terms 'majority' and 'minority' imply not so much the relative numbers in each group but the relative influences each has on the norms and values of their joint society. By definition, the term 'multicultural' suggests that we should aim not only for equality of treatment for the two groups, but also reciprocity in the interaction between them. And attention must be given not just to the curriculum for the ethnic minority group children but also to the curriculum for children from the majority group.

In this discussion the term 'curriculum' will be used as a generic term to denote all the learning experiences of the school. This broad definition will allow a consideration of both the planned and guided activities of schools and of the so-called 'hidden' curriculum. The latter refers to the experiences that are not planned and guided, but which nevertheless constitute effective learning experiences.

The curriculum model for multicultural education which will be developed here is summarized in Fig. 2.1. The strategy that will be adopted in assembling the model will identify barriers that exist to the achievement of a multicultural society within the terms that have already been discussed. The first of these in a relatively sophisticated society like ours is the general level of literacy and numeracy of its population, both majority and minority. Then a search of the literature indicates that certain problems can be identified that are particular to children of the ethnic minorities. Third, there are the inequities and the stigma that can arise from the use of culturally biased instruments and materials. Finally, are the attitudes of teachers and peer groups, and the institutional racism of the school which can prevent the achievement of the stated goals.

Teaching literacy and numeracy skills embedded in a context that is recognizable to the pupils and with which they can identify is a familiar procedure for teachers and one that is encouraged for its effects on pupil motivation and understanding, and on the transfer of skills. These real-life contexts will be much richer in a multicultural society since it embraces a greater variety of background. Apart from the selection of ethnically relevant contexts, current work on mother-tongue teaching and the effects of bilingualism also offer help in guiding the teacher. The implications of this work go beyond language teaching since the home language can be used instead of English as the medium of initial instruction without the children suffering academically, as is de-

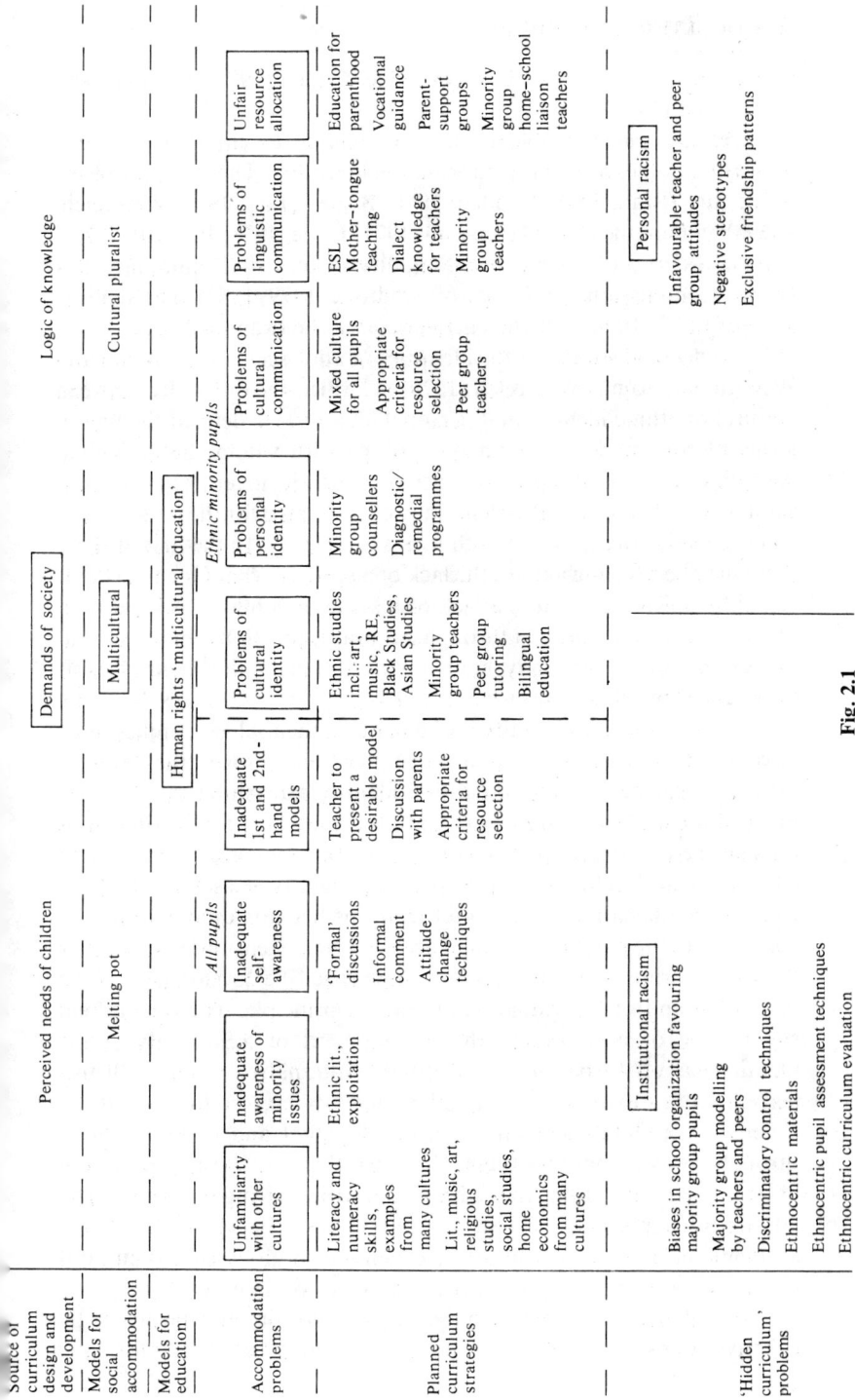

Source of curriculum design and development

	Perceived needs of children				Demands of society				Logic of knowledge

Models for social accommodation

Melting pot	Multicultural	Cultural pluralist

Human rights 'multicultural education'

Accommodation problems

All pupils				Ethnic minority pupils				
Unfamiliarity with other cultures	Inadequate awareness of minority issues	Inadequate self-awareness	Inadequate 1st and 2nd-hand models	Problems of cultural identity	Problems of personal identity	Problems of cultural communication	Problems of linguistic communication	Unfair resource allocation

Planned curriculum strategies

Unfamiliarity with other cultures	Inadequate awareness of minority issues	Inadequate self-awareness	Inadequate 1st and 2nd-hand models	Problems of cultural identity	Problems of personal identity	Problems of cultural communication	Problems of linguistic communication	Unfair resource allocation
Literacy and numeracy skills, examples from many cultures; Lit., music, art, religious studies, social studies, home economics from many cultures	Ethnic lit., exploitation	'Formal' discussions; Informal comment; Attitude-change techniques	Teacher to present a desirable model; Discussion with parents; Appropriate criteria for resource selection	Ethnic studies incl. art, music, RE, Black Studies, Asian Studies; Minority group teachers; Peer group tutoring; Bilingual education	Minority group counsellers; Diagnostic/remedial programmes	Mixed culture for all pupils; Appropriate criteria for resource selection; Peer group teachers	ESL; Mother-tongue teaching; Dialect knowledge for teachers; Minority group teachers	Education for parenthood; Vocational guidance; Parent-support groups; Minority group home–school liaison teachers

'Hidden curriculum' problems

Institutional racism

- Biases in school organization favouring majority group pupils
- Majority group modelling by teachers and peers
- Discriminatory control techniques
- Ethnocentric materials
- Ethnocentric pupil assessment techniques
- Ethnocentric curriculum evaluation

Personal racism

- Unfavourable teacher and peer group attitudes
- Negative stereotypes
- Exclusive friendship patterns

Fig. 2.1

monstrated by the work of, for example, Cohen (1975) and Rees and Fitzpatrick (1981).

Three groups of problems that are unique to children of ethnic minority families are identified from the literature. These are problems of identity (Brah, 1978; Louden, 1978; Bagley *et al.*, 1979; Weinreich, 1979a), communication (Townsend, 1971; Little, 1975; Edwards, 1979; Brown, 1979) and access to community resources (Community Relations Commission, 1977; City of Bradford, 1979, 1981). The significance of these studies for the curriculum will be examined here.

In his detailed studies of the identities of adolescents from Asian and West Indian origins Weinreich (1979b) clarified the difference between cultural or ethnic identity and personal identity. He defined the first in terms of role models or reference groups with whom the individual identifies. He then conceptualized personal identity in terms of perceived similarity with another. Problems may be generated for the person from an ethnic minority group in both forms of identity. In the first of these there may be a feeling akin to the lack of a sense of what Gordon (1964) called 'peoplehood', that is a lack of a sense of common descent with others, which is manifested through cultural expressions. In the second use of the term there may be a manifestation of the identity crisis experienced by adolescents generally in Western-type societies. Not only are these two forms of identity problematic in themselves, conflicts may also arise from their interaction: to emphasize and foster the development of a person's ethnic or cultural identity can inhibit the development of a truly personal identity since this may lead to identifications outside the ethnic group. The converse of this may also apply, for to encourage the development of the personal identity of a school child can lead to the alienation of the child from his/her domestic culture and conflict with the parents. This dual need can create tensions in school for the British primary school tradition emphasizes the development of the individual and of individuality, at least in principle. The operational significance of encouraging the development of a minority ethnic identity has yet to become an acceptable alternative to many British teachers. In its extreme form an ethnic identity may be fostered at the expense of a child's general social development and of his progress through the examination system. However, this may be the expectation of some parents from the ethnic minorities (Knight, 1981). The alternative, represented by Stone's (1981) work in which the child's academic progress is sought at the expense of both expanded cultural and personal identities, may be equally alien to many teachers.

Personal identity problems in the ethnic minorities may be helped by effective counselling. Of course such counselling takes place informally at many levels in school as elsewhere, but the developmental nature of the work of the trained counsellor has been described in detail by Hamblin (1978). Hamblin's definition of counselling is that, based on an interpersonal relationship, it seeks to get the learner to learn more about himself. If this definition is accepted, then we are led to the proposition that the pupil of Caribbean or Asian extraction may be more effectively guided in this learning by a counsellor of his own ethnic background. The counsellor must also consider adopting the role of advocate both to represent the interests of the individual pupil and to challenge the institutional racism that may be perceived in the structure of the school since these may depress the pupil's academic or vocational mobility. For the teacher/counsellor the goal of healthy self-concepts in his pupils as learners may also require carefully planned diagnostic programmes leading to suitable remedial work.

Two types of communication problem may be identified, the first of these occurs where the predominant difficulty is of a linguistic or para-linguistic nature. There may also be difficulties which arise from incompatibilities of frames of reference or schema. Some of these problems are described and investigated by Ghuman (1975) in his comparative study of Punjabi and English boys. The differences in frames of reference to schooling are highlighted by the remark of a Punjabi boy who insisted that they simply followed the instructions of the teacher, as opposed to the more questioning approach which characterized the English boys in Ghuman's study.

The dynamic equilibrium that exists between language and identity indicates another important function of language which is addressed elsewhere in this text.

The problems of communication of ethnic groups have been examined more fully at the level of the curriculum than has the resolution of problems of identity. Many strategies have been described that seem to hold a potential for improving the educational progress of children from homes where the familiar language is not the language of the school. Not only will English be required to be taught to those pupils whose performance in it retards their educational progress, there is evidence that some children benefit at the conceptual level as well as at the level of ethnic identity when they are taught through the medium of their home language. These two forms of language teaching are combined in bilingual education. Teachers should also be responsive to the subtleties of dialects, such as those used by children of families from the Caribbean. The employment of minority group teachers may also increase attainment. Some cautionary questions about the concept of achievement as it applies to children from different cultures will be discussed later in this text, since it is considerably more productive if school and home seek similar goals. There are also several problems that arise in the process of educational evaluation in a multicultural context, these too will be discussed elsewhere.

Finally, there are difficulties associated with the lack of equal opportunities. These are illustrated by the disproportionately high incidence of unemployment among black and coloured youths, by the disposition of 'immigrant' housing in run-down inner city areas and by limited educational progress as reported in some studies of black British boys. These observations are verified in many official documents in Britain such as the report of the Community Relations Commission (1977) and in various local reports, for example the Bradford Metropolitan District Council's (1981) *District Trends* and the Redbridge Council for Community Relations (1979) *Cause for Concern*. They have also become a focus for social concern during the riots of July 1981. These problems are essentially problems of unfair allocation of resources which varies not just as a function of social class, but, as Prandy (1979) argues, is also related to ethnic group.

Some of the problems outlined here are located in the school and constitute what has been called institutional racism, others lie outside the school. Given the availability of jobs, houses and social amenities the school can help alleviate some of the tensions for individual pupils wherever they may be rooted. Vocational guidance and education for parenthood, combined with improved sources of information for parents, can contribute to the process of alleviation, but may take several generations fully to resolve. Vocational guidance can assist pupils to explore a wider range of job opportunities than they might otherwise do. This should lead to more effective choice of school courses providing relevant pre-entry qualifications. Education for parenthood could enable older pupils to appraise their parents' situations more realistically and clarify the available options. These provisions could be supplemented by the establishment of parent-support groups, by the appointment of home–school liaison workers and by the development of loan schemes for books and other culture-bound materials, such as toys, sports equipment and prints.

2.6 Problems of the 'hidden' curriculum: institutional and personal racism

A legacy of the days of overt British colonialism is the feeling of superiority that persists in many of us white British. Some expressions of this attitude have been quoted in Chapter 1. The institutions we set up, including our schools, are invested with the values on which these attitudes are based. Since many of our values are ethnically linked they tend to favour pupils of the major ethnic group. But those traditional values may result in the continuation of institutions in which discrimination against pupils of different ethnic groups is found and where ethnocentric materials and forms of organization are used. This results in preferential treatment and greater success for pupils from the majority group, and a high probability of distress to pupils from the minority groups. Discrimination of this kind has been called institutional racism.

The form the hidden curriculum takes will vary from school to school and from time to time within the same school. Few schools in Britain, even in those areas of high ethnic minority concentration like Bradford or Bristol or Birmingham, will have teachers and non-teaching staff from the minority groups. Apart from the obvious representations of the views of the ethnic minorities, schools which have staff members from the minorities affirm the value of these groups. A similar affirmation arises from the use of minority group languages and dialects. For instance Chapman (1980) notes the positive effects of the use of Punjabi in school assemblies as part of the Bradford project in mother-tongue teaching. She describes the increased esteem that affects both the children of Asian origin and the indigenous children. (See also Rees and Fitzpatrick, 1981.)

Many senior schools adopt forms of grouping such as streaming and setting designed to create greater homogeneity of teaching units. The criteria that are used for the purposes of allocating pupils to groups are normally based on attainment, although occasionally behaviour and motivation are also taken into account. But, whatever the ostensible purpose of the grouping, and no matter how objective the criteria that are used, if the grouping results in a disproportionate number of pupils from the minority groups in the 'lower' sets or streams then such a system of organization can be regarded as discriminatory since the future prospects of these pupils are prejudiced. A similar argument has been used by Coard (1971) and more recently by Tomlinson (1981) as a criticism of the numbers of West Indian pupils who have been ascertained educationally subnormal.

Some methods of class control used by British teachers are culture bound, as is the level of control that is sought. Generalizations are difficult to sustain as variations exist between schools and even between classes in the same school. However, the overall ethos is one that is frequently a source of concern to parents who attended schools in South Asia or the Caribbean. They expect to accord teachers, especially male teachers, greater respect than is currently customary in Britain and encourage their children to be obedient in school. My own small-scale research in Bradford suggests that the parents of ethnic minority group children expect school discipline to be authoritarian and rote learning to be the principal teaching method. This is the mode of teaching supported by Stone (1981), herself a West Indian social worker and lecturer.

The extent to which minority group parents can prepare their children for British schools is often limited. If as a result of this the expectations formed by the children conflict with the reality they experience then cognitive and affective confusion can result. By way of illustration, my own work showed that many West Indian mothers emphasize the ritual of a child raising a hand before talking to a teacher; they also regard learning their 'ABC' at an early age as critical to a child's education. A white British middle class mother is not likely to prepare her child in this way. If the minority group child experiences a normal reception class in which children are encouraged to speak as spontaneously as they might at home, and in which play, talk and pre-reading activities predominate, then it is highly probable that he will be inhibited by his uncertainty about how to behave and the relationship that should be created between himself and his peers and teachers. The resulting hesitancy would contrast with the less inhibited responses of children whose parents have experienced a similar ethos or who will have become informed about current educational practices and who thus have a more valid and fuller range of expectations.

Syllabuses that ignore the cultures of the pupils are not unusual in British schools. The advantageous effects of using the children's own cultural context in enhancing their self-esteem has been shown in this country by the work of Dr Eric Midwinter and others. This leads to increased motivation and greater understanding of the material being taught. Not to use the cultures of ethnic minority pupils can be interpreted by them and their families as indicative of the limited worth of their cultures and, by implication, of those who cling to them.

Associated with the use or lack of use of home background within the syllabus is the teacher's tacit acceptance or rejection of varied patterns of living. A teacher's views of, say, what is an acceptable family configuration can be unwittingly conveyed to the pupils and any exceptions from that standard may be regarded as deviant, with all the consequences that the label can bring. Similar effects can ensue if teachers are unable to accept or tolerate different forms of dress, food and eating habits.

If teachers are accepted by their pupils they can become models of behaviour. By this I do not mean that they are, or become, ideal types, but rather that they come to be imitated. Several conditions attach to the process of modelling, these will be discussed later. They are not necessarily linked to ethnic groups, so in some situations white, British, middle class teachers can become effective models for children from other social and ethnic groups, thus imposing a 'colonial' influence on them. Since modelling is a valid and powerful teaching method there would appear to be no way of eliminating this effect while still preserving the teacher's influence as a teacher. However, the potency of modelling does demonstrate the need for teachers from the minority groups, if this aspect of the hidden curriculum is to remain compatible with the goal of multicultural education.

Two further examples of discrimination that can, arguably, be regarded as part of the hidden curriculum are of a more personal nature than those considered up to this point. Non-verbal cues are frequently ethnically specific. Driver (1979) has identified four sources of unwitting discrimination that arise from the misinterpretation or lack of re-cognition of non-verbal cues on the part of the teacher. He notes the persistent confusion of white British teachers over the identities of black British pupils long after other pupils are correctly identified by name. He also observes that 'West Indian' pupils tend to look away from the teacher when reprimanded, as a mark of respect, but this is frequently interpreted by white teachers as bad manners. There are also responses which are almost habits that the black British pupils use and are intended to convey specific meanings to one another. These cues include clicking, pouting and plucking the lips with the fingers. White teachers and pupils are usually unaware that these actions are intended to convey derogatory feelings. Finally, there is the use of dialect which, again, few teachers understand and, as has been mentioned previously, there is a range of communication from which the majority of teachers are excluded. There is, therefore, a limitation imposed on the participation of the teacher in the jokes and humour of a section of an ethnically mixed class, the development of empathy is inhibited and the range of techniques that may be used for class control is restricted.

Finally, let us examine 'hidden' friendship patterns which may be influenced by the organization of pupils into groups. One of the striking findings in a study by Jelinek and Brittan (1975) of the friendship patterns that may be found in junior and secondary schools attended by children of diverse ethnic groups was the low incidence of inter-ethnic friendships. When friendships only between pupils of the same ethnic group persist in schools it can convey the message that not only is integration not a goal, but that it may even be actively discouraged. But

Jelinek and Brittan sought not just the actual but the desired friendships as well. They found that at 8 years, 10 years, 12 years and 14 years of age, for indigenous children as well as for those of Caribbean and South Asian origin, the pupils desired more friends from other ethnic groups than they actually had. The researchers also looked into the barriers to friendships that might exist between ethnic groups and the following were identified: lack of facility in English; length of stay in England; cultural differences; the difficulty of changing established friendship patterns; lack of encouragement, or at worst, disapproval from society at large; discouragement resulting from the curriculum and the visual environment of the school. Much other research into friendship patterns in general has also isolated contiguity as being of crucial importance and this, too, could be an important factor in the case of ethnic choice since ethnic minority families tend to live close to one another.

The work of the Research Unit into Ethnic Relations, formerly located at Bristol University, has noted in many of its case studies the dating between adolescent black British boys and white girls. There are also descriptions in the literature of the way in which young children play together apparently totally disregarding differences in skin colour, for example those documented by Brown (1979). The picture may in reality be much more hopeful than that conveyed by Jelinek and Brittan in 1975. But even if we accept a more integrated perception of cross-ethnic friendships, if they constitute an important index of harmonious relations among ethnic groups, then again there may be unintentional aspects of the curriculum that can encourage or discourage such friendships.

Several of the barriers to friendships that have been identified above may be represented in the hidden aspects of the curriculum. These include lack of encouragement or disapproval through the attitudes of some teachers, ranging from neglect to negative discrimination. Since children frequently follow the lead supplied by the teacher, if the teacher shows his acknowledgement and acceptance of the diversity of society then the probability of his pupils following that lead is increased. Finally, grouping within a class for particular cooperative activities may ignore the possibility that ethnically mixed groups can work successfully while at the same time promoting the development of friendships through cooperation rather than competition.

Several of the issues that have been discussed have arisen elsewhere in the chapter, but here the essential feature has been the covert, implicit, 'hidden', but no less potent, nature of the reality that is experienced by pupils of all ethnic backgrounds.

2.7 Conclusion

This chapter has been written as the key to understanding, and as a justification of, this book. In it I have incorporated all the essential elements of the remainder of the text and have indicated some of the interrelationships among them. Each of the salient elements will now be considered separately in the remaining chapters; in them theoretical aspects will be outlined and practical implications will be discussed.

2.8 Summary

2.1 INTRODUCTION

Three main sources of curriculum development have been described:

The perceived needs of children

The demands of society

The logic of knowledge

Maximizing the development of the child may conflict with the aspirations of the ethnic group.

2.2 CRITERIA FOR CURRICULUM DEVELOPMENT

Some major aims of education:

The pursuit of equality and freedom in dynamic relationship

Vocational preparation

Development of the imagination

2.3 MODELS OF SOCIAL ACCOMMODATION

Key concepts from immigration theory:

Assimilation: absorption into the majority culture

Segregation: establishment of discrete communities

Integration: each group retains some of its cultural integrity while sharing services, amenities and activities with others

Models of society:

Melting pot: assimilationist

Cultural pluralist: 'unity in diversity'

Multicultural: culturally reciprocal

2.4 MODELS OF EDUCATION FOR A MULTICULTURAL SOCIETY

Human relations model: assumes that tolerance of other human beings is an inborn quality, conflicts arise from incorrect perceptions which can be changed through education.

Interracial model: token recognition is accorded to minority cultures, but children are not encouraged to consider the possibility of full ethnic equality.

Human rights model: group differences are of equal worth and minorities have a moral as well as a legal right to preserve their cultural uniqueness if they wish to do so.

A human rights model of education is consonant with a multicultural model of society

2.5 ACCOMMODATION PROBLEMS

All pupils:
    Unfamiliarity with other cultures
    Inadequate self-awareness
    Unsatisfactory first- and second-hand models
Ethnic minority pupils:
    Problems of cultural identity
    Problems of personal identity
    Cultural communication problems
    Linguistic communication problems
    Unfair resource allocation

2.6 PROBLEMS OF THE 'HIDDEN CURRICULUM'

Institutional racism:
    Disproportionately few teachers from the ethnic minorities.
    Grouping that results in disproportionate representation of minority group children in the 'lower' streams or sets, as well as in special schools.
    Methods and levels of class control are culture bound.
    Excessive gap between home and school and inadequate preparation of pre-school children.
    Lack of incorporation of pupils' culture into the syllabus.
    Rejection by the teachers of unfamiliar life styles.
    White teachers present models of the dominant culture.
Personal racism:
    Persistent confusion by white teachers in identifying black British pupils.
    Gaps in the interpretation of non-verbal cues.
    Lack of knowledge of dialects and no attempt to acquire the knowledge.
    Low incidence of cross-ethnic friendships and no encouragement given to foster the development of contacts between children of different ethnic groups.

3
Bilingualism and bilingual education: some theoretical perspectives

'What is "bilingualism"?'
'How is a second language acquired?'
'What is "bilingual education"?'
'What effects do "bilingualism" and "bilingual education" have on children?'

3.1 Introduction

An examination of 'bilingualism' and 'bilingual education' and the concepts and models related to them are crucial to an understanding of the education of children from minority ethnic groups. It can also be argued that if the term 'bilingual' is interpreted broadly, to include not just ability to use more than one language but also more than one dialect (bidialectism), then a consideration of this topic is relevant to the work of teachers of the majority of children in British schools. Because, although the linguistic medium used in formal systems of education is traditionally the language of the politically or economically dominant group, there are considerable variations, even in white British homes, from what has been called Standard English. Any child brought up in a home where this is not the day-to-day language has a barrier to overcome before he can gain access to the education and general benefits of society at large. This assertion should not be interpreted as blaming either schools or parents, but is rather a description of the situation that may be found in a large number of British schools at the present time, not just in the language that is spoken but also, and perhaps more importantly, in written language.

Harold Rosen and Tony Burgess (1980) begin their account of the language and dialects of London school children with these words:

> In the space of twenty years the configuration of linguistic diversity in the schools has been altered beyond recognition. Our school population contains large numbers of pupils for whom English is a second, perhaps third, language; there are also pupils who are fluent speakers of English but

who also speak another language; there are speakers who have in their repertoire an overseas dialect of English or a British-based form of it.

Each of these languages or dialects is used to fulfil one or more functions which the child gradually becomes aware of and refines from the early years of life. It helps to communicate needs from the marginally differentiated cries of the young baby to the complex cries of help of the adult. The use of language assists the child to become integrated into the life of home and later of school. He is comforted and comforts others in his turn through the sympathetic selection of words and their vocalization. He creates patterns of the world in his mind from the words that are provided by his social context. His social identity and his relationships with those with whom he is speaking or to whom he is writing are established and confirmed by the words that are used and the context of their use. Language has personal as well as public functions and to be bilingual is significant for the person as an individual and as a member of a social group.

The connotations of the word 'bilingual' and the forms 'bilingualism' can take are not fully clarified by reference to a simple dictionary, they will be examined in this chapter together with some models of second language acquisition and the principal models of bilingual education. I shall follow this with a general overview of some of the problems that may be met in teaching a second language, including bilingual literacy. Then some of the putative effects of bilingual education on the self-concepts and identities of children from minority ethnic groups will be considered. More specific teaching strategies and techniques will be described in the next chapter.

3.2 Models of bilingualism

A simple definition of bilingualism implies the ability to use more than one language, but this conceals a variety of possibilities regarding the forms of language that are used and the contexts in which they are brought into play. One of the decisions that should consciously be faced in schools where there are marked differences between the language of the home and the language of the school is whether to use more than one language, and if so, which language to use for which purpose. A hasty response to an issue that deserves careful thought should be avoided since there are advantages and disadvantages whichever language is chosen.

The first wave of education, or more accurately of schooling or instruction, to which immigrant children are exposed in receiving countries such as America, Germany and Britain, aims to overcome the barrier that exists when these children are unable to speak the language of the dominant group. The scope of this specific instruction is short term, that is, it is *transitional* in duration. The intention of the instruction is *assimilation* of the immigrant into the indigenous culture. Two further models of bilingualism may be identified, these are partial bilingualism and full bilingualism. In partial bilingualism the speaker is proficient in either spoken or written forms of the two languages. One form of partial bilingualism is monoliterate bilingualism, that is the person speaks both languages, but reads and writes only one. Full bilingualism is identified when the person is able to use spoken and written forms of both languages.

When the particular goals for the selected forms of bilingualism have been selected for each language that is to be used, we should then ask a series of questions:

Which variety of language should be used?

For how long should it be used?

For what purpose and for what subjects or areas of the curriculum should it be used?

By which persons should the different varieties of language be used: teachers and others?

What teaching methods should be employed both for language teaching and for general education?

These questions will be examined in more detail later in this chapter and in Chapter 4.

3.3 Models of second language acquisition

Since an adequate model of second language acquisition will point to the most effective and efficient teaching method, this section should not be regarded by the practising teacher as too esoteric to be worth the time spent on reading it. The changes in practices over the past 25 years are clearly related to changes in the explanations that have been proposed for the way in which second languages are learned; some of these will be outlined here.

ERVIN AND OSGOOD (1954)

Two models were proposed by Ervin and Osgood to describe the way in which a second language may be learned and stored in the brain. They suggested that the first and second languages can be stored as a single *compound* system, or they can be learned and stored independently of one another as a dual *coordinate* system. Other studies, e.g., Dillar

(1974), which investigated the compound-coordinate issue, viewed it as a continuum rather than as two clear-cut, separate systems. Whether one accepts the idea of two discrete models or a continuum, it is assumed that in the true compound bilingual the two languages are organized as separate systems.

It has been suggested that those who learn the second language before the age of six years acquire a compound system, whereas people who learn a second language after 13 years of age acquire a coordinate system. But age is not the only independent variable in this process. Further independent variables cited by Albert and Obler (1978) are the manner of learning the second language and the pattern of use. In one-parent, one-language situations coordinate bilingualism is produced; teaching in school using a translation method would result in compound bilingualism. In a community which regularly mixed languages people would become compound bilinguals; jet-setters travelling between monolingual societies would be coordinates. However, Riegel (1968) discussed the possibility that there may be a development from coordinate to compound systems; and the converse has been proposed, that where the use of the two languages becomes associated with particular contexts there may be a development from compound to coordinate systems.

KESSLER (1972)
From empirical evidence Kessler constructed a model that indicated that structures that are shared by two languages are acquired in the same order in both languages. In the simultaneous learning of two languages they are learned independently, and it is only when syntactic rules shared by the two languages are of equal difficulty that they are mastered in the same order.

SELINKER (1972)
Selinker proposed that when a person learns a second language he creates a unique language that falls between the first language and the target language. The new 'interlanguage' progressively approaches the target language, but some stages become fossilized and remain a feature of the language that is peculiar to the non-native speaker. The idiosyncratic nature of the second language is not the result of bad teaching but is to be expected.

DULAY AND BURT (1974)
One of the main issues in a consideration of second language teaching is whether the second language is learned in the same way as the first.

Dulay and Burt concluded from the low percentage of errors arising from the interference of the second language by the first in children that both languages are learned in a similar manner and so opportunities should be provided for children to acquire a second language in as natural a way as the first.

TREMAINE (1974)

Unlike other models discussed here this is a model of the perception rather than the production of speech. Tremaine suggests that the beginning learner processes cues such as word order and emphasis at first. He then moves on to take particular account of context in understanding, what has been described as 'intelligent guessing', based on prior linguistic knowledge. The listener has learned that word order and emphasis are significant in language processing and that greater understanding can arise from taking the context into account. The implication is that children should be taught words in a context which is relevant to them.

HARTNETT (1974)

He assumed that there is no definitive route to second language learning. Hartnett studied the relationship between second language learning and cerebral dominance. He found that English-speaking students who successfully learned Spanish as a second language through *deductive* methods, i.e., methods in which rules are taught first and then appropriate illustrations provided, seemed to be using the left hemisphere of the brain, which is normally found in first language use and is associated with eye movements to the right. Less consistent results were shown by students who were successful in a class taught by inductive methods, i.e., when structures are presented by way of conversation and the students allowed to draw their own conclusions.

ALBERT AND OBLER (1978)

Another neurological study by Albert and Obler found that although the left cerebral hemisphere is generally dominant for language, the right hemisphere may be dominant for the second language of the bilingual. The two hemispheres use different strategies for linguistic functions. Consequently, it may be helpful to develop strategies for second language teaching that emphasize the 'right hemisphere strategies' that respond to visuospatial techniques such as rhymes, music and dance associated with the language to be learned. This study complements the work of Hartnett.

No consensus has emerged on the process of second language

learning. While this may in part be due to lack of agreement at the level of the principles that may be involved, it may also reflect the variations that can occur due to differences in pattern at different ages and to differences that arise when the two languages are learned simultaneously or consecutively.

3.4 Models of bilingual education

Bilingualism is the ability to speak, or listen, or read, or write, or any combination of these, in more than one language; bilingual education is concerned not only with instruction in more than one language, but also with the use of two or more languages as mediums of instruction.

Joshua Fishman (1976), an American who has written extensively on bilingual education, has identified three models. These models are as follows:

> Compensatory or transitional bilingual education
> Language maintenance bilingual education
> Enrichment bilingual education

TRANSITIONAL BILINGUAL EDUCATION
This form of bilingual education aims to provide minority group children with opportunities to master the language of the dominant group as quickly as possible so that they are able to 'get by' within the host community. In the cases of children of school age, while they are developing a command of the target language the language of the home is used along with the 'new' language as a 'co-medium' of education.

Several problems can arise from the adoption of transitional bilingual education. It is essentially assimilationist. The child from an Asian or West Indian home may infer from the emphasis on Standard English at school that it is not just different from the language of the home but superior to it. This may result in his identification with his home and its culture becoming weakened, and the child is alienated from the support his home might otherwise have afforded him. Another difficulty that can arise is that as the dominant group language, and the education that is provided through it, are imposed on the child, the school may not gain the involvement of the minority group in the education of its children: the aims of education formulated by the home and school may be in conflict. This form of education is based on the assumption that when pupils from minority ethnic groups leave school they will be treated as the equals of leavers from the dominant group and will become assimilated as easily as they are into work and other social institutions.

This social goal may not in fact be achieved and so the preparation for life afforded by this model may become discredited.

LANGUAGE MAINTENANCE BILINGUAL EDUCATION

As the name implies, this form of education is designed to maintain the language of the home alongside the second language that is being acquired by using both as media of instruction. The introduction of the second language is controlled to match the ability of the pupil to cope with both it and the home language. Parity of use between the two languages may not be achieved until the later years of schooling. This model of bilingual education is the one most commonly found throughout the world and is favoured by nationalistic groups such as the Welsh and the French-Canadians, both of whom have gained some measure of political power despite their positions as ethnic minorities.

There are difficulties in this model. For the school leaver and for the adult in the community economic mobility may be largely dependent on proficiency in the second language; however, since only a limited time is usually spent in teaching the 'unmarked' or minority language, their command of the language of the dominant group is frequently limited. School leavers who are proficient in their home language at the expense of English often find themselves segregated from the broader community and their education is sometimes exploited for the redress of unconnected grievances. The lack of emphasis on the second language can also result in school leavers being unemployable in the wider community and this may encourage their return to the country from which their families originated.

ENRICHMENT BILINGUAL EDUCATION

This form of bilingual education has an appeal for parents of children from the dominant group, especially for those whose home language is not a major language in terms of international exchange. It is also attractive to those whose first language is English or French but who appreciate the advantages that may be gained from fluency in more than one language.

The cause of social unity would be served if dominant group parents demanded tuition for their own children in the language of one of the subordinate groups in society. For instance, in the case of Bradford children, the Punjabi language would meet this end, but since the possibilities of economic or social advantage are remote such pressure is unlikely. The major problem arising from the adoption of this model is that of making good teaching available to all who demand it in the more advantageous languages.

The acceptability of bilingual education depends on the relations that exist between the minority groups and the dominant group and on the social, economic and cultural variables that obtain in the situation. Two crucial factors are the numbers of individuals involved and the expected length of stay of the migrant minorities. Large numbers of young, minority group pupils who are expected to stay indefinitely are likely to be given transitional bilingual education unless the ethnic group can organize themselves politically to bring pressure to bear to demand maintenance or enrichment programmes. Smaller numbers of older pupils and temporary migrants generally receive maintenance bilingual education.

An analysis of models of bilingual education is summarized in Fig. 3.1.

Educational programmes	Transitional programmes	Language maintenance programmes	Enrichment programmes
Social intentions	Absorption	Separation	Addition
Associated models of society (see models of society)	Compatible with a 'melting pot' society	Compatible with a pluralist society	Compatible with a multicultural society
Comment	The first language becomes 'swamped' by the second Often rationalized as 'relocation' rather than as 'dislocation'		

Fig. 3.1

3.5   Bilingual education and the self-concept

The concepts of the self-concept and identity are defined and discussed more broadly in Chapter 5, here the interrelatedness of bilingual education and the self-concepts and the emerging identities of minority group children will be considered.

In his analysis of the development of self-concepts George Herbert Mead (1934) differentiated between the functions of the significant other and the generalized other. These two groups of entities may contribute different perspectives to the child's self-evaluation, acceptance of social constraints, expectations and attitudes. For a bilingual person it is frequently the case that the oral use of the home language is identified with significant others; the use of the second language, particularly in the form of reading and writing, is associated with the generalized other: 'them' as opposed to 'us'. If this is so, then it carries implications for the school, since the need for a closer identification with the home in other ways is indicated.

If we accept that a person's self-concept develops from his perceptions of how he is viewed by others, Christian (1976), as a result of this, maintains that a critical step in the modification of the self-concept of a child from a minority ethnic home takes place when he starts school and his name is altered. For a young child, his name and its pronunciation is an important component of his identity. If the name, or even its sound, is changed, then it disturbs the child's sense of continuity, as well as giving him a clue to the strength of the regard with which he is held by the other person. (We have all experienced some measure of discomfort related to our names. For instance, can you recall your feelings the first time you heard *your* name being used to call another person? Or the first time you were called by a nickname, or by your surname at school?) Christian tells of a friend from Mexico who attended a school in Colorado; his name was Jesus Olmos, but his teacher, when calling the register, put the surname first and called him: 'Almost—Jesus'. Berger and Luckman (1966) emphasized the significance of the name when they wrote: 'The child learns that he is what he is called'. One's imagination is strained in considering the possible effect of being called 'Almost Jesus'.

The distinction between home and school is further highlighted for the child by the probability that it is only when he starts school and begins to use the language of the school that he sees his name represented in writing, and that is usually in the language of the dominant group.

Skin colour can add to this process of differentiation. As a consequence of a black skin the minority group child can be forced into becoming a different person or a 'divided' person. A story is told which illustrates the effects of a sudden awareness of colour difference on a young child. A four-year-old West Indian girl who had lived in an otherwise all-white children's home for some three years without any visitors from her family. She was described as well adjusted, happy and sociable until her natural mother visited her one day. She cried at first that the visitor could not be her mother, but gradually over a period of days, as the staff persisted that the black woman was indeed her mother, the child became more and more withdrawn and difficult to handle. Of course this is not to say that all, nor even many, black children reject their colour in this way but it does imply that in some cases skin colour is an important dimension of identification. But this will be discussed in more detail in a later chapter.

There are two major influences which a child from a minority ethnic group encounters at school and which affect his self-concept. First is the perception that the dominant group has of his ethnic group, as it is applied specifically to himself. There may also be a developing awareness in families with only limited literacy that in-group perceptions of social reality are associated with oral language, but the out-group perceptions of reality are expressed in both oral and written forms. These influences will modify both the view he has of himself and his self-esteem, as well as his sense of his own permanence and continuity.

3.6 Bilingual education and English as a second language

In countries that are predominantly English-speaking bilingual education refers to education in and through both English and another language. Therefore bilingual education for ethnic minorities such as Asians from Pakistan or India who have recently arrived in Britain involves learning to speak English as a second language, although it would be reasonable to predict that within two or three generations in many of these families the 'language of the hearth' will be English, and Urdu, Punjabi, Hindi, etc., will be learned as second languages, as is largely the case with Welsh at the present time. At the same time, when the children leave home they may be living in three cultures at different times: a British culture at work, an Asian culture on certain social occasions and an inter-culture if the home has undergone a measure of anglicization.

Difficulties can arise in learning a second language through the 'interference' of one language by the other. 'Interference' refers to the way in which the first language can influence the word order, say, or the accent, in the production of the second language. Nevertheless, in bilingual education, because concepts of and insights into processes such as reading and writing transfer readily from one language to another, the teaching goals will tend to be common to both languages rather than language specific. Concepts do not have to be acquired twice, in most cases; when they have been introduced and understood in one language only additional labels need be added to them. Two schools of thought exist regarding the matching of the teaching of both languages in a bilingual programme: one says that concepts and processes should be well learned in one language before they are introduced in the other, while the second view is that not only should the sequencing and pacing of the material be similar, they should also be taught close together in time in both languages. There is insufficient empirical evidence fully to support either view at the present time.

The ideal staffing arrangement requires a teacher who is fluent and competent to teach in both English and the first language. But an acceptable practical alternative is a team teaching situation in which one teacher teaches in and through the home language and another teaches English, with each teacher having some knowledge of the other language. In this alternative arrangement the English teacher will have responsibility for the development of language skills in the second language and for content taught through English. The home language teacher will help the child to develop language skills in the first language, teach content through that language and provide translation for the pupils to ease their learning of and through English. For bilingual education that meets psychological as well as linguistic needs in children both teachers should have parity of status as well as acceptable competence and performance in both languages.

If a maintenance model of bilingual education is adopted, care should be taken to balance the time devoted to the two languages since the aim of the model is to establish equality in the way in which both cultures are valued. Whichever staffing arrangement is adopted, it is probably better to allocate time exclusively to one language so that interference of one language by the other is minimized.

To maintain parity between the two languages in a bilingual education programme both should be used as media for teaching/learning of curriculum content. Some ideas for achieving this are discussed in Chapter 4 where further curriculum suggestions are considered.

3.7 Bilingual literacy

Any programme of bilingual education that does not aim for bilingual literacy implies a process of assimilation and hence carries with it a discriminatory view of the minority group and its culture. This may result in the minority children assuming a position of psychological and social inferiority, or they may overcompensate in their attempts to establish their worth.

Daphne Brown (1979), in a useful text on mother-tongue teaching poses several questions, she asks:

> does the E2L child lose the values which his own language symbolises when he learns to speak English, and does he feel that he is betraying his school, his teachers and his English speaking peers when he uses his own mother tongue? How easy, or how difficult, is it for an immigrant or E2L child to identify himself with two languages and two 'classes of people'?

These questions while perfectly valid are not original since answers to similar ones have been suggested by several authorities. For instance, Fishman (1971) wrote that where there is limited literacy in the home the child becomes less convinced of the validity of the language or dialect used there and so gradually becomes assimilated into the dominant culture through identification with those who speak the language of the school. This creates a set of tensions in the child that are derived from his own preferred language, the language he actually uses due to the constraints of his social context, and the language used by his reference groups. Hertzler (1965) argued that where a person lives within two cultures he must be oriented to two different worlds, and so is a 'divided man'. And Labov put it simply that to change a person's language is to change his identity. These conclusions are not derived from empirical analyses of large samples but are clinical judgements based on detailed examination of personal experiences. They are based more on plausibility than on probability. The results are not inevitable consequences of any change of language, but they are certainly indicated if the change is forced on the child and his family.

The person who learns to read a language other than his mother tongue will have certain unique problems to overcome. When a child learns to use his first language he learns what is possible in that language in terms of sounds, grammatical structures and meanings; and he learns to reject other combinations of sounds and structures and other meanings. He learns what sounds can be used consecutively, for instance, and so the English-speaking child learns to reject the possibility that a word has no vowel sounds: not just that it is unlikely that such a word can be found, but that it is impossible to construct a word that does not contain a vowel. Again, when newsreaders on television or radio try to pronounce names like 'Nkomo' as fluent speakers of the language would pronounce them, the attempts are often regarded as affectations.

In English we learn that the definite article is followed by a noun or nominative group; in Urdu the definite article is not used. Lado (1957) provides some examples from Spanish and English by a procedure called 'contrastive analysis'. The sound of 'i' as in 'sit' does not exist in Spanish, so the child who has learned to speak only Spanish at home has not learned to hear or speak the sound and will have difficulties of language perception in distinguishing between SIT/SEAT, BIT/BEAT, SHIP/SHEEP, LIP/LEAP, FIT/FEET and so on, without guidance. When he learns to read and write in English the child must be able not only to differentiate the sounds, but also to know when to represent the 'i' sound as 'i', 'y', 'ie', 'oe' or 'ui'. If at school the child is compelled to become literate in a language other than his first language he must be taught to read, to a greater or lesser extent, in sounds and collocates that he has initially been shaped to regard as meaningless. As a result of this he is likely to encounter conceptual conflicts, or cognitive dissonance, as well as being challenged at the levels of self-concept and language.

Christian proposes that, ideally, minority group children should be taught to read and write in the home language in the pre-school years and to continue to learn the mother tongue and through it alongside the school language when they go to school. The home language can become the tool for the acquisition of literacy in the school language; the child, in this instance, 'learns to think about reading' in his more familiar language. And learning to read and write in the language of the home can confer prestige on that language.

When a pupil is encouraged to read for meaning he employs his own intuitive knowledge of the language to make intelligent guesses or predictions about the symbols in print and the sounds they represent. The more he understands the language and the context of the printed matter, the more accurate will his predictions be. The more the child can make use of his language skills to make predictions the less he needs to rely on the mediating skills of phonics and whole word recognition; the speedier recognition of words in print will result in meaning being constructed with greater accuracy and fluency from the printed word. This has a direct parallel with Tremaine's (1974) model of second language acquisition.

The child who is developing literacy skills in a second language must learn to predict from a less familiar vocabulary and syntax pattern. There may also be variations in the meanings of words he is trying to read. So, as far as possible, we should try to obtain a good match between the language of the child and the language of the reading material.

Kaminsky (1976) argues that for children to be able to read a language they must be able to think in that language. So she recommends that the child's experiences should become the basis for learning to read since this is the surest way of enabling the child to generalize his understanding of the way in which meaning can be carried either by spoken or written symbols. One method that is based on this premise is the *language experience* approach. Through this method the child dictates to the teacher, who writes the child's words, and teacher and child read back the text together. In this way, all the words and structures the child is encouraged to read will be part of his spoken language.

The most highly recommended approach to teaching, say, a child whose first language is Urdu to read in English is to teach him the initial stages of reading in his home language. This proposal is based on the premise that reading is essentially a thought process, rather than a superficially linguistic one. Once the child has mastered the process, he is more able to apply his understanding of the process to the less familiar language. But this approach carries with it implications for staffing and the availability of resources that are more fully discussed in the next chapter.

Bilingualism is desirable for social and cultural, as well as for psychological reasons. Socially it provides the bilingual person with a greater range of competence, in two environments rather than just one, and it allows access to two cultures. Psychologically it contributes to the development of the individual's identity.

Bilingual education provides tuition in two languages as well as education through them. It could be argued that fullest familiarity with a language requires knowledge of the cultural contexts of that language and bilingual education seeks to provide such a context in more than one language. It also provides a verification for the pupil of the importance of his mother tongue and the culture of the home. So it assists in confirming the child's cultural identity. Bilingual education can, therefore, play an important part in the development of the self-concepts of the ethnic minorities and their motivation to contribute to a diversified society. The specific implications of bilingualism for the classroom are discussed in the next chapter.

3.8 Summary

3.1 INTRODUCTION
A consideration of bilingualism and bidialectism is essential for all teachers.

3.2 MODELS OF BILINGUALISM
Transitional bilingualism: aims to help the newly arrived to 'get by'.
Partial bilingualism: the person is proficient in either spoken or written forms of the second language.
Full bilingualism: the person can use both spoken and written forms of both languages.

3.3 MODELS OF SECOND LANGUAGE ACQUISITION
Ervin and Osgood: draw a distinction between compound and coordinate language learning and storage; in a compound system the two languages are closely interrelated, in a coordinate system they are learned and stored separately.

Kessler: structures that are shared by both languages are acquired in the same order.

Selinker: an 'interlanguage' is formed which approximates increasingly to the target language.

Dulay and Burt: provide evidence to support the view that the second language is learned like the first.

Tremaine: the beginning learner at first processes cues such as word order and emphasis, later he takes account of contextual clues.

Hartnett: when learning is located in the left hemisphere teaching through deductive approaches is more effective.

Albert and Obler: the right hemisphere may be dominant for second language learning so visuospatial strategies may be more effective.

3.4 MODELS OF BILINGUAL EDUCATION

Compensatory/transitional bilingual education: often a temporary expedient.

Language maintenance bilingual education: both languages are used as media of instruction.

Enrichment bilingual education: adopted when advantages can be perceived by parents in acquiring a second language.

3.5 BILINGUAL EDUCATION AND THE SELF-CONCEPT

At school the self-concept is influenced by the following:

The dominant group's perceptions of the minority ethnic group, as they are applied specifically to the child.

The awareness that the in-group perceptions of social reality are associated with oral language, but the out-group perceptions are expressed through both oral and written language.

3.6 BILINGUAL EDUCATION AND ENGLISH AS A SECOND LANGUAGE

Concerned with education in and through English and another language.

3.7 BILINGUAL LITERACY

Bilingual education that does not include bilingual literacy discriminates against the language that cannot be read and hence against the culture and its people.

Bilingual literacy is best taught after literacy has been achieved in the home language.

4
Language teaching

'What can the general teacher do to help the language development of children from the ethnic minorities?'
'What language medium should be used to teach curriculum content to children whose first language is not English?'
'What are the implications of living in a linguistically diverse society for the language teaching of children from the majority ethnic group?'

4.1 Introduction

In this chapter I shall examine the major areas of language teaching in schools and describe some of the best practices that are in use at the present time.

There are two major constraints that are common to teachers in all schools, they are: every teacher feels at some time that there is not enough time to do all that should be done, and this is confirmed by the Department of Education and Science in *The School Curriculum* (1981); and teachers question their ability to solve the problems of the child with specific language needs. In response to the first constraint it will be seen as this chapter develops that a considerable part of the language work can be undertaken using the selected language as a medium of communication and thought while teaching other areas of the curriculum, as a development of the principles embodied in the Bullock Report (1975).

The second constraint can be seen as an illustration of the tension that exists between absolute standards and relative standards. Never to feel content with one's current knowledge and skills may be regarded as a sign of the professional, but since a teacher's interest in what he teaches and in the pupils who are being taught can be a powerful motivator in inducing children to learn, it is often the case that a teacher with limited understanding can still be effective in terms of the pupils' learning and their wish to continue to learn. This is not to say that understanding and professional training are not desirable, but rather that when these are not available interest conveyed to the pupils, careful observation and analysis of one's teaching and of the children's responses can lead to favourable results as well as leading to personal and professional development.

Suggestions will be made in this chapter that will be based on the assumption that it is feasible, and even desirable, to involve all teachers in language teaching regardless of the age range of their pupils and the subjects in which they specialize.

4.2 What shall we teach?

Bearing in mind the model of society on which this book is based, the answer I shall provide for the opening question of this section responds to five areas of language teaching:

The development of Standard English
Learning through Standard English
Expression through the first language
Learning through the first language
Further languages for those whose first language is English

There is an act of fine balancing required of teachers so that an appropriate emphasis is placed on each aspect of the language curriculum within the constraints of time and staff expertise. In the first place, if we recognize the dispersal of power in the community and the most well-worn routes for social and vocational mobility, then effective performance in Standard English is essential for all children. In order to achieve familiarity not just with textbook English but with content through which negotiations, such as examinations can take place, at least part of the curriculum should be taught through the English language. In Chapter 2 and Chapter 3 we have examined the important role that the home language plays in identity development and in promoting family cohesion, so there is also a strong case to be made for teaching the language of the home and to use that language as a medium for teaching other areas of the curriculum. Finally, since we are concerned for the preparation of all pupils for living both in a culturally diverse society and in a world with many diverse languages, a case can be made for teaching other languages to children whose first language is English, the so-called enrichment approach to bilingualism. The extent to which we choose to develop an enrichment approach is dependent upon a number of factors, not least are the languages that can be offered by the staff of the school and the wishes of the parents. The minimum that might be offered, on the grounds that reciprocal interest in minority cultures may carry political as well as social and cultural advantages, is a project *about* languages with children up to, say, 13 years of age. Some ideas for such a project will be described later.

INTERFERENCE

Difficulties can arise in new learning of any kind when previous learning or familiarity creates incorrect expectations. The controls on, say, a television set may be positioned differently on a new set and it may take some time before the correct choice of button can be made without error. The same principle governs the concept of linguistic interference.

Many British writers of texts on second language learning devote considerable space to a discussion of the effects of interference, but its importance is not unquestionable. In 1972 George found that one-third of the errors of adult second language learners could be attributed to the effects of language transfer, a figure which is similar to Lance (1969) and Brudhiprabha (1972). But the study of Dulay and Burt (1974) with children suggests that developmental factors cause up to 87 per cent of the errors in English as a second language in children of five to eight years of age, whereas less than 5 per cent of the errors were caused by interference. A characteristic developmental limitation described by Brown and Bellugi (1964) arises from limited memory, they regard the short length of child utterances to be due to an inability to plan ahead more than a few words at a time.

It has been assumed that contrastive analysis, that is the analysis of the difference between two languages, will enable the teacher to predict mistakes and plan the syllabus to take account of their probability, on the grounds that errors are likely to occur where there are differences between the first and second languages. But George (1972) has reported that 'learners' errors show remarkable uniformity irrespective of mother tongue'. Because of the low level of predictability of errors and the general tendency to focus attention on the learner, over the last 10 years or so linguistic specialists have developed error analysis which has tended to replace contrastive analysis. We shall consider this in a little more detail later.

Garvie (1976) and Edwards (1979) have invested interference with a great deal of importance and provide some interesting examples to support their point of view. Edie Garvie writes, 'The Urdu speaker who says "I not coming" may be confused by the fact that in his first language the presence of "not" sometimes allows the equivalent of "is" to be left out, and the one who says "My castle is big than yours" is following the custom in Urdu where the adjective itself is never altered as English alters "big" to "bigger".' But, bearing in mind the work of Dulay and Burt, it is possible that these errors are caused by developmental factors rather than by interference. Another example quoted by Garvie is the lack of a one word equivalent for 'yesterday' and 'tomorrow'. These are expressed in a phrase such as 'one day away in the past' or as 'one day away in the future'. Again there may be discrepancies in the sound systems of the mother tongue and English, as exemplified by the Asian who says 'aeroflane' and 'vindow'.

Dr Edwards makes a useful analysis of interference in writing, both in the writing of Creole grammar and in spellings which reflect the sounds of Creole. For example, the English 'th' as in 'thin' is rendered as 't' or 'd' as in 'tin' and 'tree'.

Difficulties of comprehension and difficulties of production can be caused by linguistic interference. At first, listening comprehension produces the most pressing problems since children find the instructions and other transactions going on around them confusing. But Edwards says that, as reading comprehension becomes progressively more complex, interference with the pupil's understanding becomes more serious in inhibiting progress. Dr Edwards suggests that the main impediment to language acquisition may be not so much the difficulties inherent in language learning *per se* but people's attitudes to them. She says that it is vital that teachers appreciate the differences between Creole and Standard English in order to anticipate the areas of possible difficulty and that when difficulties arise pupils' sensitivities should be protected.

DIALECTS

The primary question here is not so much whether dialects can be eradicated but should they be eradicated.

Probably the most influential answer that has been given to this question by an expert in the field was provided in a widely quoted article by William Labov called 'The logic of non-Standard English'. Since it is one of the key statements in this field it should be read by all teachers (Labov, 1972, 1973). The essence of his argument is that no language or dialect is more limited than others in its power to communicate ideas or express feelings. The other main argument lies in the enhanced social mobility that is allegedly conferred on the speaker of Standard English. There is no doubt that at one time this was so, but any listener to radio or television will have become aware of the range of regional dialects that are used by people of all social levels and in many social institutions.

Many go further and maintain as Edwards (1979) categorically states, 'regardless of motive, dialect eradication simply does not work'. But one's experience suggests that this statement is patently untrue for many people. Given the motivation, dialects have been eradicated by many and modified by many more. In fact, the term 'bidialectal' has been coined to describe those who can switch from one dialect of a language to another.

The view that predominates at the present time in educational circles is that it is rarely justifiable to try to change a child's dialect since it is wrapped up with his identity, any attempts to impose change on a child either by reward or punishment can imply a rejection of the child, his family and his cultural group. However, if there are strong reasons for doing so the emphasis should be on the addition of a further dialect rather than on the outright replacement of the original. Two further perspectives on dialect use and one strong case for an eradication policy exist. Both arguments for dialect-use espouse bidialectism. One view says that since Standard English is advantageous for all children, yet appreciating the vital motivating effect of dialect use, both the standard form and dialect should be used in school for both speech and writing. The second body of opinion argues that since the child's identity is integral with his dialect, this should be allowed in speech and in the more expressive forms of writing, but the teacher should insist upon Standard English for such formal purposes as form filling, official letters and examination responses and their classroom equivalents.

The strongest moral argument in the debate comes from the parents of children from the Caribbean. All non-standard speech has traditionally been heavily criticized in the Caribbean and attempts to encourage teachers to allow children to adopt a Creole have met with determined resistance from parents who have been brought up to regard it not as an equal alternative to Standard English and Received Pronunciation, but as the 'lazy man's alternative'. Cognizance should be taken of this point of view along with the contrasting opinion represented in the European Economic Community's Directive which states that governments within the EEC should 'promote, in coordination with normal education, teaching of the mother tongue and culture of the country of origin'. Therefore a policy of bidialectism might be adopted but only after consultation with parents.

4.3 Some principles of second language teaching

The period when language teaching was governed by the exclusive principles of 'mimicry, memorization and pattern drill' is now largely over. The theoretical justification for this approach was based on behaviourist learning theory that maintained that language was a set of speech habits learned through a process of conditioning and drill. Language is now, however, generally regarded as rule-governed, creative behaviour. To say that it is 'rule governed' is equivalent to saying that it is grammatically based, rather than habit based.

Some of the guiding principles of language teaching at the present time are as follows:

A consistent emphasis on meaning: we are concerned to develop children with knowledge to communicate, ideas to articulate and feelings to express, rather than speakers of words that are no more substantial than soap bubbles.

The association of words with the objects or activities they represent. The language that is taught should be *relevant to the child.*

Repetition is essential, but it should be interesting and meaningful to the child.

Positive motivation should be emphasized.

Gradation of the material from simple to more complex, so that difficulties are minimized.

Control, so that the child has no more to learn than he is able to cope with.

Error analysis should be used so that teaching has precision in relation to the child's requirements.

A child's general education should not be impeded during the time he is learning English.

Let us examine these principles in more detail:

MEANING

Since we aim for children and future adults who can use language fluently and creatively then language teaching should, right from the start, try to develop understanding in the children we teach.

ASSOCIATIONS

One way to achieve understanding is to link new words and phrases to the objects and activities they represent. At first this, according to developmental theory, should be done using actual materials, by allowing the children to handle the objects and perform, by exploration and imitation, the activities that are being discussed. When pupils have passed the concrete operational stage the links may be achieved by verbal associations.

RELEVANCE

Each of us has personal experiences of the motivating effects of activities when they are relevant to us. There are three aspects of 'relevance' to which thought should be given. The first concerns the relevance of the activities for the future as we predict it for our pupils, either as individuals or as cogs in a future social wheel. The younger the child the less effective will be our attempts to induce him to work for some future goals. Second, the activities may have an immediate relevance to the child, they may fill an existing need and so the child is highly motivated with little need for persuasion from the teacher. Third, an activity may be relevant to the learning of a subject. There is a danger here that, after the fashion of Hesse's *Glass Bead Game*, schools can create activities which have very little relevance to the needs of the child or to his future life, but which become part of the internal consistency of the world of school and are entirely relevant within it, although bearing no relevance to the world outside.

Instead of asking the question: 'Is it relevant?' it may be more useful, since brief discussion suggests that relevance is not too difficult to defend, to ask: 'Is it helpful?'

REPETITION

Many teachers, but especially teachers of language and mathematics, have inferred, with the passing of drills and rote learning, that repetition should be abandoned in the classroom. This is an error of judgement that has done a disservice to pupils since repetition is vital if knowledge is to become accessible in the memory. What we do not now seek is mindless repetition so that large chunks of undigested material can be regurgitated without associations other than with further links in a chain, as in the recitation of multiplication tables. Neither do we wish to bore our pupils. The professional ingenuity of the teacher is called for in devising ways for the creative repetition of what has been already understood, which will retain the attention and involvement of the pupils.

POSITIVE MOTIVATION

I have described (Saunders, 1979) in *Class Control and Behaviour Problems* how this crucial aspect of learning might be encouraged by teachers. Seven approaches were suggested there for increasing pupils' motivation to learn, they are as follows:

Inducing an appropriate mental set, i.e., helping to create an expectation of what is to follow.
Teaching through existing interests.
Increasing the appeal of the learning task.
Matching the difficulty of the learning task to the pupil's perceived ability (see 'Gradation', below).
Speeding up feedback.
Changing your relationship with the pupil, i.e., if a child is poorly

motivated you might question your relationship with him. Boosting the child's self-concept as a learner.

GRADATION

To grade what is to be learnt is an obvious principle in all forms of teaching. There are exceptions to this principle since the learner's interest in the material can enable him to transcend what, to the teacher, is excessively difficult.

Richards (1974) gave some idea of the difficulty of applying this principle of gradation to second language teaching and learning. He cites as probabilities that cognates, derivatives and 'loan' words, and similarities of structures between two languages may make elements of the new language easier to master. On the other hand, prediction of difficulty presumes that it is feasible to compare categories across languages; but since what is syntax in one language may be vocabulary in another, this may not be possible. The learner's existing knowledge of the target language will also influence the inferences he makes in further learning.

Psycholinguists have defined difficulty in language learning in terms of sentence length, time required for processing the utterance, complexity of derivation, types of embedding, number of transformations and semantic complexity. There is, however, little empirical evidence to support this conceptual analysis.

Richards makes the point that what a learner says may be determined by what he finds easiest to say, which may not be the same as what he knows and may vary from one learner to another. If the learner finds difficulty in saying 'I'll telephone you tonight', he may say instead, 'I'm going to telephone you tonight'. He also notes that the first words and structures learned tend to be over-used and may be resistant to replacement by later items; one question form that is learned early in a programme, for example, may resist replacement by more appropriate forms later. This suggests that utility may be an important criterion for the selection of the syllabus content that is initially taught in the second language.

CONTROL

The comments made about the gradation of the material apply also to the control of the task.

ERROR ANALYSIS

Many teachers of reading in English as a first language will be familiar with the concept of miscue analysis (Goodman, 1976). In using this technique the teacher notes the errors made by the reader and from his analysis of the patterns of error he plans a teaching sequence to help the child overcome these. Error analysis in language learning is closely analogous to this.

Corder (1974) distinguishes two types of incorrect language utterance. There are the apparently random errors that we all make that are due to lapses of memory, tiredness, the influence of strong emotions and other 'chance' factors, rather than to defective linguistic knowledge. We are usually aware of these as soon as they occur and can rapidly correct them. We also have errors that reveal the state of the learner's 'transitional competence' in learning a language and these errors are of a systematic nature; that is, they fall into recognizable patterns, they seem to follow rules, albeit incorrect rules, and they can be predicted.

To summarize the two types of incorrect usage:

> Random mistakes; incorrect *performance*; unsystematic; due to chance factors, such as tiredness and the effect of strong emotions. Rule governed errors; errors of *competence*; systematic, hence predictable; due to transitional competence.

Performance mistakes are of no great importance in the process of language learning. Errors, on the other hand, provide evidence of the rules the learner is formulating for himself. Their significance to the teacher, as Corder suggests, is that when the errors are analysed they can point to the progress made by the learner and to what remains to be learnt. More importantly, errors are indispensable to the learner. The making of errors can be regarded as a device the learner has of testing hypotheses about the language he is learning.

Corder quotes the following dialogue which shows how, in the course of making errors, a young child can be seen to be testing out hypotheses about the language he is acquiring.

> *Mother:* Did Billy have his egg cut up for him at breakfast?
> *Child:* Yes, I showed him.
> *Mother:* You what?
> *Child:* I showed him.
> *Mother:* You showed him?
> *Child:* I seed him.
> *Mother:* Ah, you saw him.
> *Child:* Yes, I saw him.

First the child tests out the agreement between subject and verb in the past tense; then he tests a hypothesis about the meanings of 'show' and 'see'; and third, he tests the form of the irregular past tense of 'see'. As Corder says, if the child had answered 'I saw him' immediately, we would not have known whether he had merely repeated a sentence that had been provided for him *in toto*, or had already learned the rules deriving from the three hypotheses.

The mother's function in this example is also worth noting. Only in the final part of the dialogue did the mother provide the correct form: 'You saw him'. Earlier in the conversation she simply questioned the child's utterances: 'You what?' and 'You showed him?' Merely to have provided the correct form immediately would have barred the child from generating further hypotheses for testing. Much earlier, Carroll (1955) proposed that the teacher might profitably create problem-solving situations in which the learner would be required to find appropriate verbal solutions to problems either by consulting a dictionary or by asking the teacher.

Corder argues that, whereas the first language learner has an infinite number of hypotheses to test about the language he is learning, the task of the second language learner is simpler in that he need test only the hypothesis: 'Are the systems of the new language the same as or different from those of the language I know?' and, if different, 'What is their nature?'

From this we can infer that the task of the teacher is threefold:

To look for the systematic errors that suggest limited competence and plan the subsequent teaching to help the child overcome these.
To help the child to test his own hypotheses rather than to provide answers.
To create problem-solving situations which require the child to find appropriate verbal solutions.

4.4   Strategies for teaching English as a second language

Now that we have discussed the broad areas that should be taught and some of the principles that should guide our teaching, we shall consider some details of content and method.

There are two main models of language teaching, these represent a conflation of the three approaches to curriculum development outlined in Chapter 2. The first of these is a structured approach guided by views of what are crucial, yet simple, elements of a language which should be taught first. These are built upon through a syllabus that is controlled and graded by the teacher. The second of the models relies more heavily on the effects of incidental learning on the children who are 'picking it up'. In these two models 'construction' is contrasted with 'accretion': the igloo is contrasted with the snowball.

Conventional wisdom in the British infant school in the last 35 years has stressed the importance of the child guiding his own learning, rather than having structured teaching imposed upon him. Townsend and Brittan (1972) recorded that in their survey of the organization of multiracial schools, 'a considerable proportion of schools with infants made no special arrangements for teaching English to immigrant pupils other than took place during a period when the use of the term "immigrant" was more generally applicable than it is today'.

While allowing that all children learn a great deal of language from the transactions that go on around them, many writers in this field, such as Garvie (1976) and Brown (1979), argue that incidental learning is not sufficient to optimize the learning of the child who is learning English as a second language. They claim that the quantity and quality of the language learned in this way are not satisfactory because ethnic minority children may be exposed to limited vocabularies and restricted phrases and sentences which are repeated insufficiently and incorrectly. Daphne Brown also notes that fluent English speakers in school do not listen attentively enough to non-English-speaking children and do not respond to them in ways that will encourage further language development. From a detailed study she concluded that children of five years of age and younger probably find it easier to 'pick up' a second language than a child of six years or over.

There are two further points to add to this argument. In 'picking up' language from peers there will, inevitably, be a bias towards colloquial forms; these may be acceptable, but some consideration should be given to their desirability. Second, in the early fumbling and mumbling towards linguistic competence, the older child may not have the social reinforcement from his peers that encourages him to continue, and the implications of this for class management should be considered.

Motivation to learn when structured approaches are used derives in large part from the self-enhancement effects of mastery; incidental learning capitalizes on the intrinsic motivation that is generated when children are allowed to develop their own interests.

In practice the polarization that is implied here is unlikely to exist for, no matter how structured the stated curriculum, pupils learn a great deal from informal discussion with teachers and peers. And, on the other hand, few conscientious teachers who adopt informal teaching methods would refrain from planning at least some of their work using records of a child's present performance.

I shall now outline the published schemes of Ward (1977), Garvie (1976), Brown (1979) and Holmes (1978). In addition to being a comprehensive scheme, each has something to offer the teacher who favours an eclectic approach.

WARD, G. W. S. (1977) *Deciding What to Teach*

A strategy to guide our planning, together with some useful examples, has been produced by Ward at the Arboretum Language Centre at Nottingham. He suggests that teachers should ask three questions in planning a curriculum for non-English-speaking children, they are:

1. Why do the children need to speak English?
2. What sort of sentence pattern and what vocabulary will the children need to use?
3. In which situations are the children going to need to speak English? or, What situations can the teacher use to illustrate and teach the chosen area of language?

He suggests that children may need to speak English to:

identify themselves, to ask for help, to ask for directions, to hypothesize, to explain a problem.

Answers to the second question will include:

'Can I have a . . .?' 'What's this?' 'It's a . . .' 'What does a . . . do?' Tenses of verbs, forms of questions, use of adjectives and adverbs. Lists of words compiled to various rationales; areas of vocabulary, such as parts of the body and classroom objects.

There is clearly an overlap between the suggestions but, whichever form of planning is adopted, the relevance of the work to the immediate language, educational and social needs of the children is stressed. A relevant situation would be one in which children frequently find themselves, always bearing in mind the existing language that has already been acquired by the pupils. Younger children would find great relevance in such topics as 'the home', 'shopping' and 'playing games'. Topics which would have greater relevance to the learning needs of older pupils would be 'buying a pair of jeans', 'being interviewed for a job' and 'going to the Job Centre'.

In planning the order in which sentence patterns will be taught the ability to locate objects, such as 'Where's the bus stop?' and 'Where's the loo?' are more basic than the identification of objects, as in 'What's this called?' and 'It's a . . .'.

Ward also suggests that in the early stages it is probably more relevant to teach formulae such as 'I don't understand', 'Excuse me', 'Thank you' than to teach pupils to distinguish between 'this' and 'that' or between definite and indefinite article. The following suggestions are made of the kinds of functions and situations where they may be required:

Identifying self: in talking to a teacher and to other pupils; to policemen, doctors and other official people; at an interview; in filling in forms.

Asking for help: from a teacher or other pupils; from a stranger in the street; when shopping.

Locating objects and places: in class, in school, in the street.

Possession, claiming, establishing, etc.: in the classroom, the cloakroom, in the playground.

Identifying objects and actions: objects and activities in the classroom, science lab., cookery room, art and craft room, games lesson.

Describing and comparing: in lessons such as art and craft, in map work, modern maths, in shopping.

The booklet in which this material is published is called *Deciding What to Teach*. It lives up to its title, but does not exceed it by recommending teaching methods.

GARVIE, E. (1976) *Breakthrough to Fluency*

In this book, based in large part on her experiences as coordinator of language work for children of Asian origin in infant centres in Bradford, Edie Garvie accepts a role for discovery learning when children learn English as a second language. However, she stresses the importance of the teacher helping the child to focus on a specific field of learning. She describes a 'field of learning' as the experiences in which the child is involved and the language associated with those experiences.

To guide the child's discovery the teacher must first identify the learning purposes, the activities and the materials that may be found in that field of learning. Garvie suggests that as an aid to this the school staff should, as a team, draw up a checklist of language which is used in the situations faced by the child at school. Each area of the curriculum as well as the general areas of school life must be analysed in terms of the learning content, activities and materials contained in each and the language demanded in these. It is not intended that this list should be used definitively, but simply as an occasional reminder for the teacher.

In the early stages of learning, when the verbal facility of the children in English is non-existent or very limited, Garvie suggests that a number of adult helpers are desirable so that the children can learn what is expected of them in the most rapid way. For the children, a two-way process is taking place: while acquiring language, young children are learning the concepts that are signified by that language, and learning concepts is a vehicle for learning further language. But this dual process can only take place if the teacher intervenes at the appropriate time. Along with this form of learning, the children should also be learning the language of instruction: 'Begin here', 'That's right', 'Do you understand?'

In stressing the gradualness of learning English, Garvie describes three stages which she calls 'Initial orientation', 'Cracking the code' and 'Breakthrough to fluency'. At the stage of 'Initial orientation', the children are often unaccustomed to individual freedom and so at first more time should be devoted to group activities such as movement, role play and singing. Clear instructions should be given by the teacher in a movement period and these would be followed in an exaggerated way by the other adults present.

In role play, Garvie writes, 'the aim is to illustrate behaviour patterns linked to a minimum of situational-bound language, the kind which has sometimes been described as survival language because it enables a non-English-speaking child to get by in the general sea of confusion'. Of course, it could be argued that the early language should be selected on the grounds of its universality so that it is applicable outside school and thereby increases the repetition and relevance which leads to greater mastery and heightened motivation.

The communal activities that have been described should be interspersed with periods of play with selected individual apparatus such as climbing frames, bricks and sand trays.

In the middle period identified by Edie Garvie as the period of 'Cracking the code', the first steps should be made towards literacy and numeracy, while at the same time intensifying the oral language work. The intention is to enable the child to move away from simple imitation and repetition to knowing the rules productively. More complex instructions should be given, such as, 'It's your turn' and 'May I go next?' Table games like Snakes and Ladders, Snap, and Lotto are recommended. Topic or centre of interest work can be introduced. Garvie insists that the acquisition of the second language at this stage should not be allowed to impede the child's general education. She suggests that ideally the child whose first language is not English should be taught through his mother tongue in parallel with the learning of English.

In what she calls the 'final stage of this phasing-in period'—the 'Breakthrough to fluency stage'—the child is helped to adjust to the normal pace of school work through extending and exploiting earlier work and by introducing new topics in all areas of the curriculum.

In her book Edie Garvie provides examples from the work of Bradford teachers involved in preparing their various lists of words, sentence patterns, categories of experience and so on. The completed lists may be found in Garvie (1974). Taken together the two publications in 1974 and 1976 provide a comprehensive guide to the English that young non-English-speaking children should, in her view, acquire. In addition, some stimulating ideas are provided for teaching through what may be called guided discovery.

BROWN, D. M. (1979) *Mother Tongue to English*

For Daphne Brown, headteacher of an infant school and nursery, the starting point of a lesson is of vital importance in teaching young children. She argues for a language group which is a 'positive place of learning'. Her work might be regarded as an extension of the structured, but quite exciting, teaching developed by Edie Garvie in which language is living and highly relevant since it emerges from the experiences provided for the children by the teacher.

The room in which the language teaching takes place is the familiar classroom for young children equipped with sand, water, paint, clay, bricks and home corner. As the children familiarize themselves with the surroundings and begin to use the materials they become keen to share their discoveries with the teacher. At this point the teacher introduces the appropriate English vocabulary and begins to develop it on the basis of each child's interests.

The teacher does not wait passively for a chance encounter that will provide a lead into the introduction of specific vocabulary or structure. Lesson plans include not only what should be provided and what should be taught next, but also decisions on the most advantageous positions for particular materials which will allow the 'natural' introduction of a block of work on, say, colour discrimination and naming. Two starting points which Daphne Brown has found particularly fruitful are food and clothing.

Language work arising from the topic 'food' is introduced into discussions of meals, setting the table, buying materials, as well as cooking and eating the products. Her young children have made toast, boiled and fried eggs, cooked chapatis and pancakes, made porridge and soup, jam, tea, cakes, biscuits and pies. A teaching point was developed from each of these items. For example, a group of six-year-old children who had been at school for a year did not know what toast was and referred to it as 'burnt bread'. Brown quotes the language of their teacher while two children spread butter on some toast:

> Look, Charanjit is putting butter on the toast, she is spreading butter on the toast. Harmesh is putting butter on the toast, he is spreading butter on the toast. What are they doing? She is spreading butter on the toast. He is

spreading butter on the toast. They are spreading butter on the toast. How many pieces have they spread with butter?

Making and eating the toast became an acceptable and meaningful vehicle for the repetition of language to which the children had already been introduced. At the same time the children were being introduced, probably for the first time, to the concepts of 'toast' and 'spreading'.

Another interesting example from this programme is making porridge. This activity is accompanied by the teacher telling the story of the Three Bears. In this way 'too lumpy', 'too hot', 'too salty' and 'too cold' are not just learnt as verbal tags, they are simultaneously experienced by the children.

The importance of careful planning to enliven the introduction of new ideas and the associated words is illustrated during a breakfast prepared by the children for the school caretaker. He opened a jar of marmalade which the children did not recognize. The teacher asked them from what it was made. When they were unable to guess its contents she told them that marmalade was made from oranges and produced, like a conjurer, an orange from her pocket. This allowed the children to associate the various elements in reality, rather than simply in mental images.

The principle of repetition is emphasized by Brown. She writes of the importance of reinforcing the same phrases and repeating the same language patterns and words in different situations.

Teachers will recognize in Garvie's and Brown's suggestions many of the elements of what is now considered to be good infant practice.

HOLMES, J. (1978) '*Sociolinguistic Competence in the Classroom*'
Sociolinguistic competence is the ability to use language appropriately in a wide range of social situations. Janet Holmes, in Australia, illustrates this from the reported work of Ervin-Tripp (1972) and Sachs and Devin (1976). They record that, when talking to babies, even two-year-old children use the intonation of baby talk and children of three and four years use shorter, grammatically less complex, utterances to children who are younger than themselves.

School is a novel social situation for children who enter it for the first time. It is a formal setting in which they are expected to participate fully. There are certain sociolinguistic constraints that govern formal classroom interactions and these impose particular problems on children from minority linguistic and cultural groups. Holmes describes some of the constraints that are imposed on children from minority groups and suggests ways of alleviating the problems that they induce. She also indicates ways of developing sociolinguistic competence in a second language.

As a contrast to the traditional classroom learning style imposed on children in British schools, Holmes refers to the description Phillips (1972) gives of the methods of learning that are employed in the American Indian, Warm Springs, culture. First, there is a relatively long period of silence during which the children listen and look at what is being taught through demonstration. Next, the children cooperate with and are supervised by an older relative in carrying out a segment of the task. Third, there is a period of self-initiated testing, unsupervised and in private, until the child feels ready to demonstrate his new skill to others. Very little speech is involved, in contrast to schools where there is an emphasis on answering teachers' questions about skills rather than in performing them, and this is often required before an opportunity is created to watch others or for private practice.

The observations of Driver (1979), Khan (1979) and my own research (Saunders, 1973), all of which are referred to in more detail elsewhere in this text, have indicated that minority groups differ in the expectations they hold for schooling in this country. These variations can cause misunderstandings in the classroom. For example, Lein, cited in Cazden (1975), found that black American pupils frequently misinterpreted their teachers' instructions and she concluded that these derived from two kinds of response they had learned to make to their parents. She described the situation in these terms:

> 'Reasonable' commands, such as 'You can't go outside now, it's dark', are immediately obeyed. But commands without obvious justification, like 'Wipe that smile off your face', or 'Come stand over here by me', are treated differently. The children understand the latter quite correctly as invitations to engage in a routinized verbal game in which the children resist, the adults repeat, with escalating insistence until they appeal to higher status members of the family or community to enforce the command. The game often lasts fifteen or twenty minutes, and everyone understands it as such.

When this kind of 'game' is transferred to school, teachers label the children 'defiant'.

Janet Holmes has recognized two advantages for second language teachers in possessing knowledge of the sociolinguistic norms of the children they teach: it helps the teacher to avoid unnecessary conflicts, and it is useful when devising teaching material and techniques. She makes several teaching suggestions as alternatives to traditional question and answer lessons. However, she reinforces the important general point that these suggestions may not be appropriate for all pupils, as formal teaching situations are sociolinguistically normal for only some. (There is also psychological evidence that pupils who are highly anxious favour structure and precise instructions and achieve 'better' results under such conditions; low-anxiety pupils favour unstructured teaching styles.) She reminds us that there is no 'best' method for teaching children who speak English as a second language to achieve the two key goals of sociolinguistic competence:

> To be able to speak appropriately in different situations.
> To be able to interpret the social meanings of utterances.

To provide linguistic diversity within the teaching approaches, Holmes recommends the following:

> Visits to places of interest; involvement in community work, weekend camps, etc. These expose pupils to 'natural language use' in a variety of situations.
> The development of pupil–pupil 'participant structures' either in small groups or in one-to-one situations which encourage cooperation instead of competition and the use of a more colloquial form of language than is normally used in the traditional classrooms.

Holmes cites evidence from Tarrant (1977) that pupil-led groups use fewer closed questions than teacher-led groups. Small groups also provide opportunities both for the use of a greater range of speech functions than is possible in a full class and for exploring ideas, interpreting information, hypothesizing, evaluating, arguing, challenging, disagreeing, etc., and to use language tentatively, speculatively and exploratorily. She goes on to suggest that minority group children need to recognize the functions of such questions as, 'Who's making that noise?' in the classroom, as well as the implications of such threats as, 'I hope I won't have to remind you again'. That is, questions and statements that carry culture-laden nuances should be taught. Further insights into the kinds of difficulties experienced by pupils who are learning to read in English as a second language are provided by Kennedy (1973). A 13-year-old girl was asked to underline words or phrases she did not understand in a history text, she underlined the following constructions:

> . . . not quite half of the population were affected by the epidemic . . . In the villages, the inhabitants were to be found sick and dying in the open . . . It stayed that way for days . . . The control of the disease was beyond them.

The problem illustrated by this example is that unfamiliar words can always be located in a dictionary, but familiar words in particular contexts can prove difficult to understand.

A further suggestion made by Holmes in discussing productive rather than receptive sociolinguistic skills is derived from the work of Labov

(1973). She recommends that a minority child might be helped to acquire 'those verbal routines of mitigation which would make it possible for him to object and refuse without major confrontation'. Other language functions that should be taught are ways of responding to a false accusation and ways of refusing a request for assistance, e.g.,

> No, it wasn't me. I was (outside).
> No, it wasn't me. I was (asleep).
> No, it wasn't me. I was (working).

And

> No, I'm sorry but (I'm too (tired) right now).
> No, I'm sorry but (I'm too (busy) right now).
> No, I'm sorry but (I have to (finish this) first).
> No, I'm sorry but (I have to (see Mary) first).
> No, I'm sorry but (I have to (wash my hands) first).

Second language learners may also need help in establishing principles for selecting appropriate forms of mitigation and politeness which depend on accurately assessing one's relationship to the other person, the formality of the setting and so on.

4.5 Teaching reading in English as a second language

Based upon her experience of teaching in a reading centre in America, Thonis (1970) has produced a comprehensive guide to teaching reading to speakers of English as a second language. In it she favours the language experience approach which should be used with children who have already been introduced to reading in the mother tongue.

Eleanor Thonis describes in some detail the introductory activities to which children whose mother tongue is not English should be introduced, these include the following specific pre-reading activities:

1. Ability to hear and discriminate the sounds of English.
2. Ability to hear rhymes in English words.
3. A minimum speaking vocabulary of 2500 words.
4. Knowledge of the sound–symbol correspondences in English.
5. Recognition of such English language cues as singular to plural, present tense to past tense.
6. Understanding of simple directions in English.
7. Ability to carry out simple commands given in English.
8. Development of acceptable English pronunciation.
9. Ability to form written letters of the English alphabet.
10. Enjoyment of simple stories told in English.

All of these, together with the traditional pre-reading skills.

Thonis also makes some suggestions for an individualized approach to reading. She recommends the language experience approach in the earlier stages then, in addition to all the general features of individualized work, she makes the following specific points:

1. Keep detailed records of language strengths and weaknesses; exploit the strengths and remedy the weaknesses.
2. Monitor the growth of skills.
3. Try to widen the child's interests by offering reading material across a broad range of subjects.
4. Read a summary of an exciting story to arouse the child's curiosity, then let him read the story alone.
5. Assign a few capable readers who are native speakers of English to help the children who may need assistance.
6. Tape-record some favourite stories and encourage the non-native English speakers to follow the story in a book while they listen to the tape. Also tape-record a person of the opposite sex from your own so that the child hears English spoken by a variety of voices.
7. Acquire stories from the countries of origin of the ethnic minority pupils.
8. Avoid long written assignments based on the readings.

4.6 Aspects of mother-tongue teaching

For as long as 'mothers' use a language or dialect at home which differs from that of the school the responsive teacher is posed with the problems: 'What do I do about it?' 'Is it to be ignored?' 'Should I try to ensure that the pupil is taught through the language of the home?' If we answer in the affirmative to the first or third question we are then forced to consider the questions: 'How much?' 'When?' and 'By whom?'.

The importance of the mother tongue has been discussed in Chapter 3, but a more personalized account is given by Khan (1979). She maps out the complexity of the motives of parents in seeking mother-tongue teaching for their children. Khan regards it as a means of:

ensuring communication with their children (in the linguistic and cultural sense), communication with grandparents, etc., in the homeland, a prerequisite for marriage, settlement in the homeland, religious instruction and avoidance or resistance to Western culture and values. . . . Work permit holders (e.g. Spanish, Turkish, Greek) have an added insecurity and uncertainty of place of final settlement. Whereas many Asian migrants have British passports, some categories of the population are orientated towards the homeland and others who planned to settle in Britain have become increasingly aware of the rejection and prejudice to be faced by their children. Certain exiled populations (the Eastern Europeans, Cypriots and East African Asians) may in fact feel a greater concern than voluntary migrants to preserve traditions.

The motives that have been identified by Verity Khan underpin the firm assertion of the Bullock Report, *A Language for Life* (1975), that:

> No child should be expected to cast off the language and culture of the home as he crosses the school threshold, nor to live and act as though school and home represent two totally separate and different cultures which have to be kept firmly apart.

A directive issued by the European Economic Community in February 1976 on the *Education of Migrant Workers' Children* stipulated that provision should be made for:

> organising and developing a reception system which would include intensive study of the language or languages of the host country . . . in addition to providing more opportunities as appropriate for teaching these children their mother tongue and culture, if possible in school and in collaboration with the country of origin.

In 1977 a revision of the Directive (77/486/EEC) removed the element of compulsion and the legal right to mother-tongue teaching; it was then accepted by the British Government. Such Directives bind the member states to the achievement of the stated goal, but leave the means of achieving it to each national authority.

Since that time there have been few attempts at clarifying the basis on which mother-tongue teaching should be implemented. Two experimental projects have been established at Bradford and at Bedford. The first was funded by the Department of Education and Science and the other by the European Economic Community. A headmistress at one of the Bradford schools involved in the project, Mrs Linda Chapman (1980), has reported her own very favourable evaluation of the project as it was carried out in her school. The intention of the project, she writes, was 'to make substantial use of a child's mother tongue, as well as English, in the classroom'. The children in this study were all five years of age, or thereabouts; entrants to the school 'with little or no ability in the use of the English language, and whose mother tongue was Punjabi (or regional variants of it)'. The criteria for evaluating the project were based on the child's adaptation to school, his acquisition of English and his general cognitive development. A more technical evaluation has been published by the project directors Dr Olav Rees and Barré Fitzpatrick (1981).

Given the success of the project, the organization of the teaching is of particular concern to us here. There were two groups at Mrs Chapman's school with an English-speaking teacher and a Punjabi-speaking teacher, with an English-speaking nursery nurse and a Punjabi-speaking nursery nurse. She describes the organization thus:

> Half the teaching time of the week was used for teaching in the English medium in which the whole group of thirty children were regarded as a single unit, and all four staff worked with all the children on a rotational basis, so that total overall contact was made between adults and children. The activities undertaken followed, as exactly as possible, the 'normal' range of activities to be found in a typical school week. In the other half of the week the children were divided into their subgroups to work separately—one group in the English medium, the other in Punjabi. . . . There was at no time, of course, any written work in Punjabi.

Two questions will immediately come to the mind of the general teacher: How can I, a monolingual English teacher, cope with the diversity of languages and dialects in my class? and, How can I give children from the ethnic minorities the attention they need, in view of the relatively ungenerous staffing ratios at the present time?

Daphne Brown has outlined some useful procedures for the ordinary class teacher. She suggests the following points:

> Every child in the class should be encouraged to speak in his mother tongue for some part of the school day.
> Parents should be invited to school to contribute to group work and school assemblies in their own language.
> Arrangements should be made with a nearby senior school for older pupils from minority groups to visit the primary school on a regular basis to tell stories in Punjabi or other relevant language.
> Assistants with a facility in a minority language should be appointed where possible.
> Minority group children who attend Saturday or evening schools in their own language and culture may be encouraged to bring their work to the day school where it can be talked about and encouraged.

Daphne Brown advises that when admitting to school children who do not speak English the following suggestions should be borne in mind:

> When instructions are given, non-English-speaking children will always be slower to respond.
> They will be bewildered by changes of routine, so explanations may need to be continued over a longer period.
> In situations where English is spoken the English-speaking child

65

will dominate and the non-English-speaking child will need added support and encouragement.

They should not always be placed in groups with less able children.

They may never have used clay, paint or dough, etc., and may be afraid of soiling their clothes.

Their parents may not expect them to move around and play at school.

Their parents may not understand work or messages sent home.

4.7 Peer group tutoring

This form of organization has a long history in education. Planned child–child tutoring has been recorded for many centuries, for instance in India in the eighteenth century, in England in the nineteenth century and in the one-room Canadian schools of the present time. Of the advantages indicated in the literature, the impact a structured approach to mutual help on the socialization, cognitive, linguistic and identity development is particularly relevant to the present discussion. From the evidence collected by Goodlad (1979) it seems that 'cross-age tutoring', in which older children help younger ones, may enhance both identity and learning in children from minority groups and be helpful to learners and tutors.

By way of illustration, when a nine-year-old Asian boy helps a six-year-old there are many advantages for both children:

It forces the older child to review what he has already learnt and repeat basic skills he might otherwise be reluctant to repeat.

If the older child were expected to exercise the basic skills alone, he would be socially isolated while doing so.

He might view the repetition as punishment.

He might not spend time on parts that required most attention.

The younger child is more likely to reveal his difficulties.

The children can use the mother tongue or English as they please.

Goodlad also makes the point that having something unique to contribute always makes the tutor more interested in the task. So, whatever the focus of the tutoring, it is important to encourage the tutors to bring teaching materials they think the tutees will value. In the context of the present discussion they should be complimented for bringing materials with an ethnic bias.

4.8 Language project

Here are some ideas for a project that is designed for the whole of a culturally mixed class. The activities that are described are intended to help children to develop an awareness of the range of languages and dialects that can be heard in Britain, often assumed to be a monolingual country. Since the ideas given here represent activities for a wide age and ability range of pupils individual teachers will find it necessary to select from the list that is given.

By adopting a broad area of work such as in this proposal a range of activities can be prepared which can free both teacher and pupils from the predictability and limitations of formal work and yet protect the teacher from having to cope with a wide variety of demands that can ensue from permitting free choice to the pupils. I shall describe the project in two parts, the first will be the teacher's preparation, then I shall outline the pupils' preparations.

TEACHER'S PREPARATION
1. Detailed purposes:
   To introduce pupils to the diversity of dialects and languages, with particular emphasis on the local community.
2. Introduction of the project to the class, to be selected from the following:
   (a) Illustrated talk by the teacher.
   (b) Visiting speakers from different ethnic groups.
   (c) Audiovisual exhibition of spoken and written languages.
   (d) Visits to focal points in the community to listen to local accents and languages, e.g., market, community centre.
3. Development of the project:
   (a) Grouping the pupils based on one of the following criteria: friendship groups, groups of mixed diverse forms of speech, ability groups—mixed or homogeneous.
   (b) Communications: workcards, tape-recorded instructions, briefing and de-briefing sessions.
   (c) Sources of pupils' information: local informants, either in or out of school; tapes and records; books; radio and television material.
   (d) Recording and collating the material; written records, tape-recordings, role play and simulations with mimicry; other oral contributions, e.g., short talks.
4. The end product, presented either in or out of school:
   (a) Exhibitions.
   (b) Role play performances.

67

1. Make a list of the advantages of knowing more than one language. Are there any disadvantages? What are the advantages of knowing more than one European language? What are the advantages of knowing one or more Asian languages?

2. Using thick wallpaper, draw and cut out a large tree with eight branches, this represents the Indo–European languages. Label the eight branches, one for each of the main language groups: Albanian, Armenian, Balto–Slavic, Celtic, Greek, Indo–Iranian, Romance, Germanic.

    Twigs can be added to the branches to represent the individual languages, e.g., Balto–Slavic: Bulgarian, Czech, Polish, Russian, Serbo-Croat.
    Celtic: Breton, Cornish, Irish and Scots, Gaelic, Welsh.
    Indo–Iranian: Bengali, Hindi, Persian, Punjabi, Urdu.
    Romance: French, Italian, Portuguese, Rumanian, Spanish.
    Germanic: Danish, Dutch, English, Flemish, German, Norwegian, Swedish.

    If words can be discovered in dictionaries, encyclopaedias or from other sources in any of these languages, they can be written on 'leaves' and attached in the appropriate positions on the twigs.

    What languages can you discover that do not belong to the Indo–European 'tree'? For example, Chinese (Sino–Tibetan), Hebrew (Hamito–Semitic), Hungarian (Ural–Altaic), Japanese (Japanese and Korean).

3. Language survey. The pupils can undertake a local survey to discover the range of languages and dialects that are used and have been used in the local community. Some of the areas for investigation are the following:
    Place names and their derivations.
    Origins of surnames.
    Languages and dialects spoken within families.
    The information can be recorded initially on lists, on maps of the locality and selective tape-recordings can be made.

4. Numbers in other languages. Prepare a chart with the numbers from 1 to 10 written in a column down the left-hand side. Pupils can complete further columns in other languages. Other practices, such as those used by shepherds can also be recorded (See Jake Thackray's recording of *Old Molly Metcalfe*.)

5. The use of symbols. On another chart, symbols other than numbers can be listed by the pupils, for example, traffic lights,

road signs, and, musical notation, chess symbols, chemistry formulae.

6. Secret languages. A variety of these can be discovered, or invented, e.g., morse code. Other examples devised by children can be found in Iona and Peter Opie's book *The Lore and Language of Schoolchildren* (OUP, 1959).

7. Sign languages. Probably the best known sign languages are those used by the deaf. Children can research into these and a user of one of them can be invited to school to demonstrate its use, preferably with a suitable partner.

8. Writing systems. There are three basic writing systems, they are alphabetic (Arabic, Cyrillic); syllabic (Japanese); pictographic (Chinese). Other writing systems have been developed for special purposes, such as the raised symbols used by the blind. Examples of each of these can be sought by the pupils.

9. Body language. Discuss how we communicate and express ourselves through our bodies. The following activities can be used to explore our use of body language in day-to-day situations.

   Personal space: have the pupils vary the distance they stand from others during conversations. What is the effect on oneself and others of standing closer than normal? Further away than normal?

   Eye contact: with the pupils in pairs, have one talk while the other averts his eyes, what is the effect of this on both parties? Try the effect of staring fixedly at the person who is talking. When both partners have taken up both roles, stop and discuss. Are there any discernible differences across cultures? Across people of different status?

   Facial expression: have the pupils explore the effect of saying something with an inappropriate expression on their faces. For example, 'I found a five pound note on my way to school', with a sad expression; 'My pet dog died this morning', with a smiling face; 'Do you want to buy anything from my shop?', with a snarl. Are there facial expressions that seem to be universally appropriate? Are there any expressions that seem to vary across social and ethnic groups?

10. Collect greetings cards from different cultures. Remember that some cards such as Christmas cards are ethnocentric.

11. Discuss the advantages of an international language. Obtain examples of such attempts as Esperanto, allow the pupils

opportunities to find out how easy they are to read, although not necessarily to translate.

At the lowest level these activities can permit pupils to practise gathering, assembling and collating information. But if children's interests are fired, opportunities can be created by this kind of study which will lead to the cultural reciprocity that multicultural education seeks.

4.9 Summary

4.1 INTRODUCTION
Common constraints on teachers:
Lack of time
Insufficient training
The concept of language across the curriculum is supported here.

4.2 WHAT SHALL WE TEACH?
The development of Standard English for certain purposes.
Learning through Standard English.
Expression through the first language.
Learning through the first language.
Further languages for those who have already acquired English.
Interference can arise when a language already acquired creates incorrect expectations in learning a second language.
Dialects: it is rarely justifiable to try to change a child's dialect.

4.3 PRINCIPLES FOR SECOND LANGUAGE TEACHING
Emphasize meaning.
Associate words with what they represent.
Make the language relevant.
Repetition is essential.
Emphasize positive motivation.
Examine gradation and control of the material.
Develop error analysis as a teaching technique.
Do not neglect a non-English speaker's general education.

4.4 STRATEGIES FOR TEACHING ENGLISH AS A SECOND LANGUAGE
Structured teaching
Incidental learning
Some language schemes:
Ward (1977) *Deciding What to Teach.*
Garvie (1976) *Breakthrough to Fluency.*

Brown (1979) *Mother Tongue to English.*
Holmes (1978) 'Sociolinguistic competence in the classroom'.

4.5 TEACHING READING IN ENGLISH AS A SECOND LANGUAGE
Thonis (1970) recommends a language experience approach so that reading is based on the child's interests expressed in what he talks about, with an emphasis on meaning right from the start. An introduction to the reading process in the first language is recommended, transfer of an understanding of what is involved eases learning to read in the second language.

4.6 ASPECTS OF MOTHER-TONGUE TEACHING
The principles on which it is justified are supported by the Bullock Report and by the EEC.

4.7 PEER GROUP TUTORING

4.8 LANGUAGE PROJECT

5
Identity, self-concepts, minority group children and the teacher

'Why are the concepts of identity and self-concept important for teachers?'

'What is the particular significance of these concepts for multicultural education?'

'What are currently important views on the implications of identity and self-concept for teachers?'

5.1   Introduction

This is probably one of the most contentious areas of multicultural education since we are concerned here with the innermost feelings of people. The problematic nature of this discussion is seen in a crude form in the following questions:

How far should a teacher go in trying to mould children to fit a pattern of his own making?

Or, to put it in another way:

Should teachers in British schools try to nurture the identities and self-concepts of children from families of, say, Bangladeshi origin along with English, Welsh, Scottish, Polish, Italian children from both working and middle class families?

If the answers to these questions are in the affirmative, then the next question must seek to establish priorities:

How central is the answer to the development of the curriculum? What are the techniques that can be used to enhance the identities and self-concepts of the pupils?

Since the answers we give as teachers to these and related questions are of crucial importance to the quality of the education we provide in a multicultural society, and as there is no consensus view at the present time, it is essential that alternative perspectives from which decisions can be made are considered by all teachers. A personal theory can then be constructed which will inform and justify the actions taken at classroom level.

One must consider the personal as well as the professional significance of identity and self-concept. For example, I write this chapter in the certainty that you have reflected on at least some of the following questions: Who am I? What am I really like? How do others see me? Would I feel differently about me if I thought others viewed me differently? Would I behave differently if I felt differently about me? Am I the same 'I' in every situation? Do I feel a member of a racial group, or an ethnic group, or do I feel myself to be an unique individual in all important respects? Or does each of these aspects contribute to my feeling of who I am? Again, am I recognizably the same person as I was in early adulthood and youth?

That you have considered some of these questions, or similar ones, underlines the fascination and subjective importance of these ideas; they also demonstrate one's ability to reflect on oneself. Such questions help us to articulate the sense we make of our lives. We weigh the information we get about ourselves from social interactions, and, in relation to the value we place on those interactions, we add to the picture of ourselves and the evaluations of that picture which each of us constructs from birth. One of the major universal goals of life seems to be to develop a personal wholeness, a sense of unity about what we do and how we appear both to ourselves and to others. Since an understanding of identity is relevant to any answers we give regarding our purposes in life and the extent to which we feel we are achieving them, if we are to understand the behaviour and feelings of members of the ethnic minorities it is essential that we consider issues related to the identities of people from these groups.

5.2 Structure of self-identity

In order to achieve some consistency in this section I write with the following stipulative definitions in mind:

> Self-image: the description, or 'picture', or 'map', I have of myself.
> Self-esteem: the value I place on the components of my self-image.
> Self-concept: this is a combination of my self-image and self-esteem, it carries a descriptive and an evaluative component.
> Self, identity and self-identity: a sense of personal continuity that combines all the self-concepts, as well as unconscious identifications and perceptions of one's capacities.

William James (1890), one of the pioneers among psychologists, took up the ideas of the eighteenth-century philosophers who recognized that man has the ability to see himself and to reflect upon what he sees. In the same way that we view others as objects and assess them, so each of us can become an object to himself and make an assessment of himself as an object. These ideas have been developed principally in America through the work of such psychologists as Allport, Maslow and Combs. Important areas of concern within this tradition have been the qualitative research and thought that has concentrated largely on our evaluations of self; on the notions of self-esteem or self-worth; on the motivational effects of high self-esteem and on the presence or absence of a sense of control which we may have over our lives. Psychologists have traditionally viewed the formation of identity as an unfolding of characteristics, stage by stage, in the way that is described by Freud in his theory of psycho-sexual development, or by Erikson who describes eight ages of man. In both of these influential theories an in-built sequence can be inferred and it is only in the activation of each stage of development that social influences come into play. Development is, by implication, orderly and hence predictable.

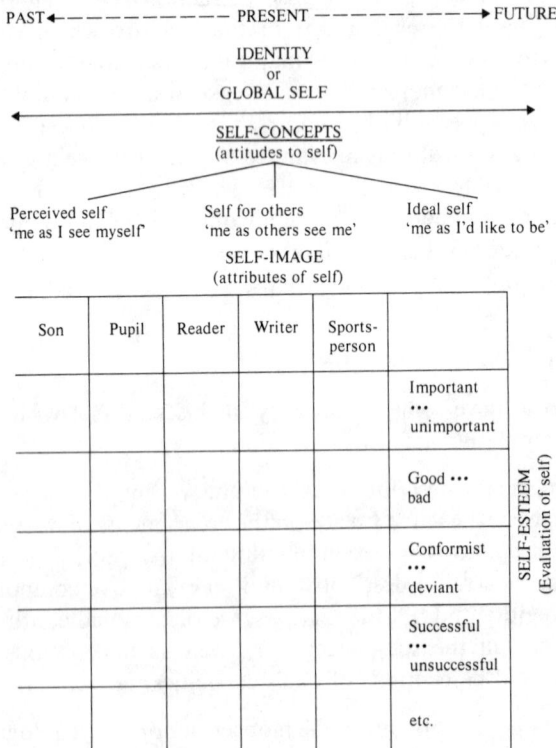

PAST ◄ — — — — — — — — PRESENT — — — — — — — — ► FUTURE

<u>IDENTITY</u>
or
GLOBAL SELF

◄───►

<u>SELF-CONCEPTS</u>
(attitudes to self)

Perceived self   Self for others   Ideal self
'me as I see myself' 'me as others see me' 'me as I'd like to be'

SELF-IMAGE
(attributes of self)

Son	Pupil	Reader	Writer	Sports-person		
					Important ••• unimportant	
					Good ••• bad	
					Conformist ••• deviant	SELF-ESTEEM (Evaluation of self)
					Successful ••• unsuccessful	
					etc.	

Fig. 5.1

Another strand in the study of the complex that is self-identity comes from the sociological tradition. Charles Horton Cooley (1902) and George Herbert Mead (1934) developed the principle that the self develops through social interaction, rather than from a predictable unfolding. To illustrate this point Cooley used the metaphor of the looking-glass: the reaction of another to a person is like that person looking into a mirror; the responses of the other are selective, and the selections he makes result in me recognizing certain characteristics and not others in myself.

Figure 5.1 is a representation of the structure of self-identity, it is a crude attempt to represent two-dimensionally the various parts of what we perceive ourselves to be. The persistence of identity over time is represented by the horizontal line stretching from past through present into the future. Each of us has a vast number of attitudes to ourself—our self-concepts—which are made up of a description and an evaluation of the attributes that we recognize in ourselves as a result of seeing their reflection from others. I see myself as a certain kind and quality of teacher, husband, etc. But this is too gross a model, for I see myself as I believe I really am (my perceived or actual self); I also have a view of me as I believe others see me (self for specific others and self for generalized others); and I see a 'me' as I would like to be (ideal self).

Burns (1979), in a review of research and theories of self, describes five main sources which inform a person of his attributes, which he then evaluates according to the standards he has incorporated from those who are significant to him. These sources are as follows:

Body image: my physical appearance.
Child rearing practices: how I am handled as a child, how I am talked to, controlled, etc.
Language: the emphases that are implicit in my domestic language.
Interpretive feedback from the environment.
Identification with the appropriate role model and stereotype.

These are not five discrete sources, each contributing a separate view of the self; they are interdependent influences that inform and guide the development of the multi-faceted picture a person develops of himself and the attitudes that are related to that kaleidoscopic picture. The nature of the feedback from each of these sources will be developed at relevant points in this text, but it will be clear that if, say, my skin colour is viewed by others as a significant difference between them and me, it may become an important component of my self-image. Whether it enhances or diminishes my self-esteem will depend upon whether my colour is the same as or different from that of a social group that is important to me.

For Erikson (1968) the process of identification was central to the formation of identity. He postulated that identity formation 'arises from the selective repudiation and mutual assimilation of childhood identification' (p. 158). But the process is not regarded as an all or nothing process; Erikson says that 'children at different stages of their development identify with those part aspects of people by which they are most immediately affected'. That is, the young child will identify with those aspects of another person that are most relevant to him at a particular period in time. During the process of socialization, the child synthesizes all his previous identifications with those who have been significant in his life and creates from them a particular view of himself. This is more than simply a process of accretion, as a person's identifications may well be incompatible with one another.

A major component of identity may be expressed in terms of the ethnic group to which he feels he belongs. The saliency of this ethnic identity is recognized here and a distinction will be made between ethnic identity and personal identity.

5.3 Ethnic identity

The saliency of ethnic identity is not an absolute for all human beings, experience suggests that each of us can be placed somewhere along a continuum between a state in which we might be totally indifferent to the group into which we are born, alternatively we might be at the polar opposite where our allegiance to our ethnic group is of desperate importance.

There are two ways of conceptualizing ethnicity, or ethnic identity. One is to regard it as a fixed characteristic ascribing membership of a group on the basis of family descent and separated from other ascriptive groups. Some of the ascribed ethnic groups in Britain at the present time include the four indigenous groups as well as Pakistani, West Indian, Polish and so on. One school is reputed to have representatives of 50 ethnic groups among its pupils. The characteristics of these groups are explained by reference to their cultural values. To permit, for example, a Sikh bus conductor to wear a turban, or a Scottish soldier to wear a kilt, are seen by many as concessions to their ascribed ethnicities. The Sikh and the Scot need to wear their own unique apparel *because* they are born Sikh or Scot, and so the wearing of the ethnic symbol carries with it certain non-rational feelings.

The other approach to ethnicity has been called a situational approach. From this perspective a person's self-identification is viewed as problematic, that is, it is not an absolute attribute but a variable one that can be subject to debate. In Wales a Welshman may define himself principally in terms of his occupational and marital status. If he does have a more specific criterion of reference he may define himself as an inhabitant of a particular village or town. Similarly with a Pakistani: before his migration to Britain he may have defined himself as a shopkeeper, a husband, and a father. He may have come to Britain to improve the standard of living of his family. On settling in Bradford or Birmingham, he and his wife may have experienced difficulties of communication with others in the community and they may have felt a need for support from others with whom they could share discussions of common problems. Insights into the working of political pressure groups would demonstrate to them the effectiveness of the ethnic pressure group in commanding a greater share of the economic resources of this country. In this case the wearing of a turban by a Sikh could be attributed to a conscious, rational decision to maintain the husband's identification with a group representing his birthplace and the culture of his childhood.

The first view of ethnic identity, the ascriptive model, is of a static attribute that is conferred on the individual without him in his turn doing anything to acquire it. The situational model views ethnic identity as a product of social interaction. Cynthia Enloe (1980) has described the difference in the models in this way:

> Ascriptive definitions of ethnicity take account of cultural dimensions of ethnic groups, but culture is secondary to the fundamental descent element linking members to one another. Cultural attributes are thought to be objectively observable and passed down from generation to generation, so that the differences in values, mores and symbols which form the social boundaries between insiders and outsiders can persist over long periods of time. (p. 4)

> Social scientists who lean towards a situational interpretation of ethnicity contend that ethnic identities are more fluid than was earlier imagined. As a consequence, their research strategies have had to be less purely descriptive and more designed to cope with interactional dynamics. (p. 5)

This is not to say that situational theorists do not subscribe to the idea of common descent linking ethnics within a situational framework. Nagata (1974), for instance, found that ethnic groups hold to a 'myth of common descent', that is they have a feeling of common descent that may not be supported by biological evidence. The importance attributed to this myth can vary with the demands of the immediate situation. She describes how a Malayan Muslim may identify himself as an 'Arab' under certain circumstances, and 'Malay' under others. This is not simply uncertainty or ambivalence but is regarded as an example of ethnic adaptability. It may, too, be akin to what Musgrove (1977) has referred to in his discussion of changes of identity arising from positions of marginality in society, that is, at times of change of social role. Nagata also makes the important point that when ethnic consciousness diminishes it does not so much 'die' as 'lie in hibernation', to reappear when ethnicity again becomes a politically significant influence.

Yancey et al. (1976), discussing the absorption of migrants as described by 'straight line theory' (assimilation proceeding in a straight line without any deviations or interruptions), argued that ethnicity in America at the present time exists because it has a survival value in present-day society. But Herbert Gans (1979) makes the point that a comment such as that made by Yancey and his colleagues applies more to the poorer ethnics, 'who have been less touched by acculturation and assimilation than middle class ethnics'. However, he describes a return to ethnicity by third and fourth generation middle class Americans which has been called 'voluntary ethnicity' by Novak (1976) and, in a more specific way, 'public Jewishness' by Bock (1976) and which Gans (1979) called 'symbolic ethnicity'. Gans maintains that for third and fourth generation Americans ethnicity has lost its instrumental functions in people's lives; it is no longer useful for earning a living or for regulating family life. Ethnicity, he argues, is now taking on an expressive function becoming, as it were, more of a leisure activity in which certain symbols of ethnicity are abstracted from the traditional culture and practised in the pursuit of identity, while people's daily lives are governed by more pragmatic considerations which are essential for bringing up a family and holding down a job. This is the connotation Wesker has placed on Jewishness in the quotation in Chapter 1.

Symbolic ethnicity can take many forms. Many Jews have emphasized the rites of passage into adulthood. Not only do they celebrate the Bar Mitzvah for the passage from boyhood into manhood, a parallel ceremony with no traditional religious validity, the Bas Mitzvah, has been invented by American Jews to celebrate the passage of 13-year-old daughters into womanhood. Easily prepared ethnic foods are another source of symbolic ethnicity. Even sending money back to the 'old country' can be a form of symbolic ethnicity if the financial sacrifice is not too great.

It has also been pointed out that a person is unable to identify with some people without rejecting aspects of others. So, it is argued, a child cannot continue to identify with the culture of his parents without rejecting at least some of the culture of his teachers and peers.

Alternatively, he identifies with the culture of the school only by sacrificing his allegiance to the culture of his home. This is a major dilemma in arriving at an acceptable teaching strategy, about which there will be further discussion in the next section.

5.4 Adolescent search for identity

Conflicts arise when a person perceives that he shares and approves of certain attributes of another person or group, while at the same time sharing yet rejecting other attributes of those others. This process has been called 'identity diffusion' by Erikson (1968). Peter Weinreich (1979a) has proposed that the resolution of conflicts of identification should be regarded as part of a natural, universal process and that it is through the active resolution of conflicts of identification that a person grows. For example, if I recognize the fact that I am a Welshman and regard musicality as a favourable attribute, an area of positive identification is indicated. If, at the same time, I perceive certain characteristics of the Welsh, say a fondness for gossip, as unfavourable, this contra-indication will create for me a state of conflict or identity diffusion.

Much of the 'search' of adolescents, from the ethnic minorities as well as adolescents generally, can be interpreted in a similar way. The clothes one wears can make a significant contribution to one's identity, particularly in adolescence, and at all ages they can signal one's identity. This can be problematic for those ethnic groups whose identities find expression in particular forms of dress. The conflict that can be created in Asian adolescents by parental restrictions has been commented on by Louden (1978). On the one hand they identify with many of their parents' attributes and values, yet wish to be dissociated from them in matters like wearing Western dress and dating members of the opposite sex. This feature of conflict is also discussed by Avtar Brah (1978), in the course of which she quotes an Indian boy who said, 'I think of myself as an Indian, but I don't like a lot of Indian ways'. This and other replies from her respondents are summarized by Brah when she concludes that they 'reflect the essential dilemma of a young person growing up in a racially or ethnically divided society. On the one hand they are not uncritical of certain features of their parents' culture. On the other, they seem to sense the danger of over-identification with the majority group which ranks their culture in a position of subordination.'

In any cultural context adolescence is regarded as a period of particular stress by Erikson and others. During this period an adolescent becomes aware of the changes going on within his body. Through these changes an identity is formed which is based on the construction of a set of values, and from this a feeling of personal unity and continuity is forged despite the problems of conflicting identifications. But the process of reappraisal is clearly not confined to adolescence. Each of us, to some degree or another, adopts new beliefs and life styles as our existing beliefs are challenged and our potentialities are realized. Musgrove (1977) has illuminated this point of view in his study of marginality. There is some evidence that many Asian parents are gradually changing their views as their children face the pressures for conformity to Western life styles.

Children brought up in a relatively homogeneous culture will be much less exposed to conflicting, contradictory identifications with persons and values than a minority group adolescent who is likely to identify across cultures. When such a person identifies with someone or with an attribute from outside his family culture, identity diffusion may be generated as he tries to reconcile his conflicts. The interlocking nature of identity means that, at times of reflection, incompatibilities between the characteristics of people will arouse conflicts when comparisons are made. But, as Weinreich (1979a & b) has recognized, a certain amount of identity diffusion is normal since it indicates a healthy questioning of one's attributes and of one's position *vis-à-vis* one's cultural group. However, high identity diffusion indicates difficulties in the formation of a sense of integrated identity, while a lack of identity diffusion implies a retreat from reality to a position of defensive high self-esteem.

5.5   Pupil behaviours related to self-concepts

In her critical review of the literature on the self-concept, Ruth Wylie (1961) produced evidence to suggest that the following behaviours were dependent on the self-concept:

> Performance in learning tasks.
> Self-regard and adjustment.
> Self-acceptance and acceptance of others.
> Self-regard and ethnocentrism.
> Self-regard and level of aspiration.

From this list it is clear that teachers should acknowledge and understand the vital part played by the notion of the self-concepts of children in contributing to our understanding of their motivation to learn, as well as to understanding children's behaviour at school. It is not an educational frill which is emphasized by impractical humanitarians, but a real tool in stimulating insights into the dynamics of learning.

One of the important questions for teachers is: Do the self-concepts of ability affect academic achievement, or does academic achievement affect the self-concepts? The first premise is the basis of what has been called 'self-enhancement theory'; the second is found in 'skill-development theory'.

Self-enhancement theory argues that self-concepts influence the level of performance, so, to improve academic achievement levels the self-concepts of ability of pupils must be made more favourable through various forms of feedback, such as counselling and reinforcement. This is the theory that is implicit in the work of Lawrence (1971, 1972) in Britain and Brookover *et al.* (1964). The latter study in America investigated over 1000 12-year-olds. From it Brookover and his colleagues estimated that a positive self-concept can account for about one-third of academic achievement. That is, the self-concept is an important, although not sufficient, factor in successful achievement. They suggested that enhancement of self-concepts can be achieved by the following methods:

> Increasing parental evaluations of their children's performances and efforts.
> Having an 'expert' inform the pupil of his ability.
> Creating a significant other, such as a counsellor, whose high academic expectations and evaluations might be internalized by the pupil.

Of these methods, the first was found to be most productive: as parental perceptions changed in a positive direction, so too did the self-perceptions of the pupils. However, the improvement was not maintained when the treatment ended. The implications of this work for the education of minority group children is that the parents should be encouraged to comment favourably on any success their children might achieve at school. And the parents, in their turn, should be supported by teachers whose appraisals and evaluations of the children they teach should be as favourable and as consistent as possible. Of course, this depends on the consonance of the aims of parents and teachers so that each adopts similar criteria for establishing what is to be regarded as success.

Those who support the skill-development model claim that the self-concept of ability is a consequence of academic attainment. In this approach individualized instruction, which recognizes a pupil's strengths and weaknesses and preferred learning styles, is the key to enhancing the child's achievement; this in turn leads to enhanced self-concepts. Perceived evaluation and feedback follow as a consequence of achievement and help to modify the self-concept of ability, rather than preceding the achievement in an effort to boost the self-concept. This model is supported by Wylie's (1961) tentative conclusions. From her review of studies of experimentally induced success or failure she found that, under certain conditions, the subjects of these experiments changed their self-evaluations.

5.6 Teaching strategies

The view is taken here that the identities and self-concepts of the pupils we teach can guide and sustain their learning and behaviour in school. Consequently, the teacher has a duty to respond to pupils to optimize their learning in any ethically permissible way available to him. It is in this respect that the teacher should be concerned for enhancing the self-identities of his pupils.

Guidelines can be drawn up to help us in directing the curriculum. The context of the discussion will be the curriculum seen as 'the child's experience of school'. This will include the attitudes of teachers, which can have a facilitating effect on the self-identities of pupils. Interrelated with the attitudes of school staffs is the organization of the school; organization may be the outcome of attitudes, and attitudes can be influenced by the organization of the school. Pastoral support is offered by one person to another in most human institutions. Here I shall briefly discuss this informal support as well as providing a guide to more professionally committed counselling. Finally I shall describe some aspects of the formal curriculum, including syllabuses which can enhance the self-identities of pupils from the ethnic minorities.

A matrix has been constructed in Fig. 5.2 showing the relationships between each of these 'experiences of school' with cultural and personal self-identities. In the more detailed discussion that follows it will be seen that each strategy may make, at the conceptual level, more than one contribution to the enhancement of self-identity.

PEER GROUP TEACHING
Reference has been made to the use of peer groups in language teaching. Its effects on the pupil-tutor have been noted by Sinclair Goodlad. Based on the work of Geiser (1969), who found that the self-concepts of 10-year-old boys improved through being given the task of tutoring, Goodlad suggests that by requiring tutors to live up to the responsibilities they have been given, tutoring develops in them feelings of high self-esteem. To this may be added the respect and even admiration of younger or less able pupils who are helped.

| | CULTURAL IDENTITY AND RELATED SELF-CONCEPTS | | PERSONAL IDENTITY AND RELATED SELF-CONCEPTS | |
	Self-enhancement	Skills development	Self-enhancement	Skills development
Attitudes	1. Peer group teaching 2. Modelling 3. Effects of teacher self-concepts	1. Mother tongue teaching	1. Effects of teacher self-concepts	
Organization	1. Segregation v. integration		1. Segregation v. integration	
Pastoral support	1. Counselling 2. Modelling 3. Building home-school links	1. Peer group teaching	1. Modelling	1. Remedial guidance 2. Peer group teaching
Syllabuses Teaching Methods	1. Permeation strategies 2. Peer group teaching 3. Modelling 4. Ethnic studies 5. Accentuation of speech markers	1. Mother-tongue teaching 2. Peer group teaching 3. Effects of mastery of material	1. Peer group teaching	1. Peer group teaching 2. Remedial teaching 3. Effects of mastery of material

Fig. 5.2

Acknowledging the work of Klaus (1973, 1975), Goodlad has described five models of peer group tutoring:

Interactive pairs
The monitor system
Unstructured tutoring
Structured tutoring
Semi-structured tutoring

Interactive pairs
Children are frequently paired off for learning tasks in class. To turn this form of grouping into tutoring requires the teacher to provide each pair with tasks of mutual instruction. Children can read aloud to one another; able pupils can be paired with less able pupils; children can check each other's work. If pairings are made on the basis of ability, thought given to the ethnic backgrounds of the pupils can lead to enhanced feelings of self-esteem in children from the ethnic minorities.

The monitor system
The use of older pupils as monitors is recorded by Lancaster in 1805 to combat the unrealistically large classes of the last century. A class can be divided up into manageable groups and monitors assigned to each group to supervise the completion of work set by the teacher. The teacher is then released to give more concentrated attention to a small

group. Again, consideration of the ethnic backgrounds of the monitors can lead to enhanced feelings of self-worth in them and a recognition of the ethnic groups they represent.

Unstructured tutoring
Considerable freedom is given to older pupils in this model in their efforts to help younger pupils. The benefits of this method include not only the gains in self-esteem that can accrue to the tutors, but also the greater understanding of the material that is to be taught that results from being forced to organize one's ideas in a communicable form. Gaps in the knowledge of tutors are quickly revealed. Goodlad asserts that the bigger the gap in age and experience—the greater the information gap—between tutor and tutee, the better unstructured tutoring is for the tutee; the narrower the gap in age and experience, the better for the tutor. Again, for our purposes the ethnic background of the tutor should be a prime consideration.

Structured tutoring
Tutors with only limited ability can be effectively trained to administer highly structured programmes. The responsibility of the tutor is diminished in this model since the material is organized for him.

Semi-structured tutoring
Here there is an attempt to combine the advantages of structured and unstructured tutoring. Tutors guide their tutees through a planned syllabus, but are free to modify it in the light of their own skills and perceptions. This model avoids feelings of insecurity that can arise if tutors are completely free to structure the material themselves and tutees are protected from the possibility of incoherence when material is badly presented.

In each of these models special consideration should be given to the ethnic mix of tutors and tutees. The cultural identification of both can be enhanced if the process is perceived to be one in which the ethnic group is valued. Gains in personal identity can arise if the worth of the individual is established. Of course, the two processes need not be mutually exclusive.

MODELLING AND THE USE OF ETHNIC GROUP MEMBERS
The use of teachers of the same ethnic group as the pupils can enhance the prestige of the ethnic group and the cultural identities of the pupils if they have a wish to be like the model and the model's behaviour demonstrates feelings of high self-esteem. Other pupils with high

prestige can fulfil a similar function. Modelling is distinguished here from imitation by the flexibility with which the learner reproduces the learned behaviour: inflexible repetition results from imitation; flexibility is a product of modelling. Modelling as a teaching technique is commonly used in the learning of skills, but attitudes to the self as well as values associated with ethnic group and life styles can also be influenced by modelling.

Waller and Gaa (1974) note seven variables of the model and of the relationship between the model and the pupil.

The model should possess a high degree of competence, status and control over resources. This is a power variable in which the learner can attribute more worth to the copying of behaviour demonstrated by someone high in perceived power or prestige.

Successful modelling is more likely to occur if the model is someone with whom the pupil has a warm, rewarding relationship.

Persons who are central to the life of the child are more likely to be used as models.

The influence of the model is increased the more the child perceives himself to be like the model.

The use of several models all exhibiting similar behaviour will tend to be more powerful than a single model.

When the behaviour of the model is consonant with that of the group of which the pupil is a member or to which he aspires, the influence of the model will be increased.

If the behaviour of the model produces consequences that are seen to be positive, the pupil is more likely to model that behaviour. If the model receives what is regarded as a negative outcome for his behaviour (say, low self-regard) then the influence of that model is diminished.

TEACHER SELF-CONCEPTS

Teachers who are high in self-esteem tend towards confidence and low anxiety, thus creating a classroom atmosphere in which pupil self-esteem and performance flourish. Teachers who are low in self-esteem tend to reduce the opportunities in class for building up personal relationships. Burns (1976) showed that progressive teaching methods tended to be related to high teacher self-esteem, while traditional methods were related to low self-esteem. High self-esteem is also positively related to acceptance of others.

Burns (1979) argues that since self-attitudes are learned they are modifiable in a favourable direction. To achieve this modification he recommends that teachers engage in group sensitizing processes and counselling procedures. Jersild (1955) suggests that such procedures may not be necessary since teachers can gain insights into their own self-concepts by posing to themselves such questions as the following:

Do I regard myself as a finished person, or as one who is still growing?
Do I possess flexible self-assurance?
Do I tolerate diversity of point of view?
Do I see myself as a person able to accept positive criticism as part of my personal and professional development, and openly discuss my personal and professional problems?

The assumption that lies behind questions such as these is that self-understanding leads to self-control, which includes control over the direction of one's development. A teacher with high self-esteem creates positive expectations for the pupils he teaches and induces them to form higher self-esteem.

SEGREGATION VERSUS INTEGRATION

The findings of studies on the effects of segregating pupils generally in special classes or special schools is by no means unequivocal. The conclusions of many who have studied the self-concepts of black pupils, however, suggest that when they are insulated from contact 'in essentially black worlds' the self-esteem of black adolescents as a group 'is not as low as one might otherwise expect'. But such segregation may result in decreased opportunities and unjustifiably low expectations by their teachers. Consonant with the aims of multicultural education, the practice that is promoted here is that of integrated schools and classes where there is an absence of discrimination.

COUNSELLING

Counselling has been defined as a process whereby a person gets to know more about himself: his feelings, needs and aspirations. Two specific aims of counselling for older pupils from the ethnic minorities are:

To help in resolving problems of identity diffusion.
To encourage self-enhancement.

There is some evidence that while these aims may be more readily achieved when the counsellor matches the ethnic group and sex of the adolescent who is seeking help, it is also the case that some pupils from minority ethnic groups more readily disclose their aspirations to white British counsellors.

Counselling as sympathetic listening has been successfully demonstrated by Lawrence (1971, 1972). Using untrained but sympathetic women who were prepared to chat with children on a one-to-one basis he showed gains in the self-concepts of the children which led to improved reading achievement. It appears that the children were able to express their emotional problems in a supportive atmosphere and developed greater self-confidence. There is also evidence from America which indicates that group counselling enabling discussions of self and of personal performance can also be effective in releasing adolescents from self-doubt and in boosting self-concepts.

HOME AND SCHOOL RELATIONSHIPS

As with several of the strategies described in this chapter there are many reasons for building links between home and school. Here we are concerned with the feelings of worth that can be engendered when the school initiates visits to the homes of pupils. At first these visits must be preceded by a request to the home from the headteacher for permission to visit, since religious constraints may prevent the mother receiving a male teacher in the absence of a chaperon.

My own cross-cultural study of the homes of educationally subnormal children (Saunders, 1973, 1977), using only a small sample of homes, indicated that the majority of parents welcome visits by a representative of the school; it also suggested that all parents, Asians, West Indians and white British, are greatly concerned for their children's education. This perception is supported by Midwinter (1977).

For the purposes of this chapter there are two main aims in initiating and sustaining these visits:

> The direct aim of boosting self-esteem by conveying a positive wish to meet a child's parents.
>
> An indirect aim, to help the parents to recognize the child's educational strengths and encourage them to praise the child for his efforts.

In addition to these aims it may be necessary for both teachers and parents to educate one another, the teacher learning about child-rearing practices and taboos of the parents' culture, and the parents learning about the advantages of, say, play.

Teachers should try to avoid over-generalizing on the basis of the limited sample of homes which they will visit since even a modicum of sensitivity and experience will reveal substantial differences not only between Muslim and Sikh homes, but also between working class and middle class homes within each ethnic group.

87

PERMEATION STRATEGIES

The view is held here that multicultural education should take place across the curriculum. In the same way that all teachers are being encouraged to regard themselves as language teachers, so all teachers must see themselves as having a positive role in relation to multicultural education. Not only should teachers' attitudes be non-discriminatory, all syllabuses should respond to the diversity of our society. This approach can be justified on several counts, here we are concerned mainly for the self-enhancing effects of permeating the curriculum with responses to diversity.

The curriculum can include discrete elements of ethnic culture, such as Black Studies and Asian Studies, but permeation is regarded as a more effective means of conveying the importance of cultures other than one's own. To implement this policy all teachers should attempt to fulfil the following suggestions:

Present the points of view of other ethnic groups.

Indicate ethnocentric or racist perspectives when they arise in the opinions of pupils, books, etc.

Use criteria in selecting books in all subjects that will exclude heavily biased materials (see Chapter 7).

Illustrate lessons with audiovisual materials which show different ethnic groups; and tapes, films, etc., in which a range of accents are used.

In lessons such as maths examples of problems should be provided that are set in a variety of cultural contexts.

An occasional word of praise in a pupil's first language or dialect can be used, perhaps more naturally with younger children.

Note special days in each child's life, either personal days, e.g., birthdays (for personal identity), or religious festivals (cultural identity), and mention them to the whole class.

Remember that ethnic groups are not homogeneous and all children need to be treated as individuals; there is much evidence (see Thomas, 1980) to indicate that teaching/learning is most effective only when the teacher personalizes his relationships with pupils.

Remember there is a close relationship between teacher expectation, pupil behaviour and learning, so monitor your unrevealed expectations for each pupil in your care.

Become informed of the values, attitudes and life styles of other ethnic groups, especially those in the classes you teach.

Don't make a public issue of some of the prohibitions of ethnic minorities, e.g., food and dress.

Check your behaviour: does it convey a belief in the superior worth of whites?

ETHNIC STUDIES

Ethnic Studies lie outside the terms of reference of the present book since they are specialist studies. It is, however, pertinent to note that enhancement of cultural identities of pupils is their chief function in the curriculum.

SPEECH MARKERS

As discussed in Chapter 4, minority dialects and languages can be used to maintain identity. An empathic movement towards the listener is indicated when the speaker tries to match his speech to that of his audience, accentuation of difference signifies a movement away from the listener.

MOTHER-TONGUE TEACHING

Teaching the mother tongue was discussed in Chapters 3 and 4, in the context of this chapter it is perceived as a form of speech which recognizes and marks off the cultural identity of the pupil.

EFFECTS OF MASTERY

There is now an extensive literature on the relationship between self-concept and achievement. The bulk of the evidence leads to the conclusion that the key to educational achievement is the experience of repeated success. This increases feelings of worth and reinforces appropriate study habits and effort. While this should not be taken to mean that the possibility of failure must always be removed from any work set, nevertheless it does mean that all children should experience success more often than failure, especially in the early stages of learning. On the other hand, the work should not be so easy that the pupil does not experience a real sense of achievement on completing a task.

REMEDIAL TEACHING

If progress is inadequate in the early years of schooling by reason of inappropriate teaching or for reasons inherent in the child, it may be necessary to engage in precision teaching of a diagnostic-prescriptive kind on a one-to-one or small group basis. Because of the difficulty that sometimes arises in differentiating between learning difficulties that are the result of an inadequate language match rather than of inadequate conceptualization, remedial teaching can be delayed. There is no reason to suppose that the normal techniques and procedures of remedial teaching could not be used with effect.

89

5.7 Conclusion

In this chapter I have tried to show the dual nature of the task with regard to self in which teachers must engage in teaching children from minority ethnic groups, and the paradox that is at the heart of this task.

Evidence has been provided in support of the view that individuals of low self-esteem are less likely to succeed in school than those of high self-esteem. Success tends to be rejected by pupils of low self-esteem if they believe it must be repeated.

Two forms of self-identity have been distinguished in pupils of minority ethnic groups, the first is that constellation of views of self which leans heavily on positive identifications with the ethnic group; the second form comprises all the positive identifications with those attributes and entities that are not associated with the ethnic group. It has been suggested that there are occasions in school where one can only be promoted at the expense of the other. This inherent dilemma is illustrated in a case in Bradford between the local education authority and some Asian parents. The case was reported in the local newspaper (*Telegraph & Argus*, 14 April 1981) in these words:

> it was common for children to be taken back to the Indian sub-continent for three months. Some were away for as long as six months or a year.
> Under schools' regulations of 1959 children are allowed only two weeks' absence for holidays outside normal school holidays.
> . . . Asian parents wanted their children to absorb Asian culture and keep in touch with their roots. But this posed problems for the children being swapped between cultures. Parents did not fully appreciate the need for an uninterrupted education if their children were to do well in exams.

Given that both groups are trying to act in the best interests of the children, there is no unquestionably correct decision to be made in this case. Yes, the children's education is being disrupted and their assimilation into British society impeded. But, on the other hand, the children's cultural identities are more readily retained and enriched; and the parents may have no wish for their children to become assimilated. Yes, they may not be so successful in examinations. But, if the number of racist acts being perpetrated against ethnic minorities increases the children may be grateful for having retained something of the culture of their parents so that they might return to their 'home' countries on a permanent basis.

The balance of the argument must, surely, result in the abandonment of a legalistic approach to problems such as this. Each case should be treated on a personal basis, giving due regard to the implications of the decision for all the individuals and groups concerned.

5.8 Summary

5.1 INTRODUCTION

Identity and self-concepts motivate pupil learning and behaviour.
Cultural identity is formed from identifications with one's own ethnic group.
Personal identity may be formed from identifications from outside one's ethnic group.

5.2 STRUCTURE OF SELF-IDENTITY

Self-image is the descriptive component of one's self.
Self-esteem is the evaluative component of self.
Self-concept is a combination of self-image and self-esteem.
Self, identity, self-identity are synonyms for the sense of personal continuity.

5.3 ETHNIC IDENTITY

Ascriptive ethnic identity is conferred on the individual; it takes account of the culture of the ethnic group as well as of descent; it assumes a relatively static view of ethnic identity.
Situational ethnic identity is flexible, its strength varies with the context.

5.4 IDENTITY IN ADOLESCENCE

Problems of identity diffusion may arise from conflicting identifications.

5.5 PUPIL BEHAVIOUR AND SELF-CONCEPTS

Self-concepts influence the following:
   Performance in learning
   Self-regard and adjustment
   Self-regard and regard for others
   Self-regard and ethnocentrism
   Self-regard and level of aspiration

5.6 TEACHING STRATEGIES

Peer group teaching:
   Interactive pairs
   Monitor system
   Unstructured tutoring
   Structured tutoring
   Semi-structured tutoring

Modelling and ethnic group representatives
Teacher self-concepts
Segregation versus integration
Counselling
Home and school relationships
Permeation strategies
Ethnic studies
Speech markers
Mother-tongue teaching
Effects of mastery
Remedial teaching

6
Negative stereotyping

'Isn't stereotyping simply a kind of concept and as such is part of the way we normally think?'
'Why is it essential that teachers understand the process of stereotyping?'

6.1 Introduction

The concept of stereotyping was introduced in Chapter 2 but since it is crucial to the expectations that we build up for our interactions with others, we shall examine it more fully here. We shall begin by taking another look at the definition of stereotyping and then consider some of the main arguments against stereotyping. Then, because we teach children in their formative years, it is important that we understand how stereotypes are formed in that period before moving on to consider how we can approach the correction of negative stereotypes. Finally, I shall discuss current understanding of stereotyping and teacher expectations.

6.2 What is a stereotype?

The concept of stereotyping was first popularized by Lippmann (1922). He defined a stereotype as a factually incorrect simple description of a person or group resulting from illogical, rigidly held reasoning. Katz and Braly (1933) regarded a stereotype as a fixed impression which conforms very little to the facts it is supposed to represent and is the result of defining first and observing after.

Examples can be quoted from many children's books to illustrate the points already made. For instance, several studies of the treatment given to North American Indians have shown that common epithets used to describe them in school textbooks are: *savage, cruel* and *barbarous*. There is a disproportionate emphasis on the North American Indians' supposed predilection for massacring, scalping and boozing.

Stereotypes are commonly believed to be associated with hostility towards certain categories of people. In their analysis of stereotyping Seccord *et al.* (1976) recognized three components of stereotyping. They said that we first identify a category of people, like students or policemen. Then we agree that the people in that category share certain traits, like bathing irregularly or exercising an authoritarian personality.

Finally, we attribute those traits to everyone in that category, however clean or benign they may be.

But stereotyping is not always hostile. Saenger and Flowerman questioned 450 American students about their dislike of certain human groups. They also asked the students for descriptions of these groups since the researchers predicted that the dislike would be rooted in these characteristics. This, however, was not the case. They ascribed to Jews, for instance, many of the characteristics they also ascribed to groups they did not dislike. Jews were described as mercenary by 31 per cent of the students, but 24 per cent described Americans similarly and 38 per cent believed businessmen were also mercenary. But Jews were more often disliked for this quality than either Americans or businessmen. Stereotypes may, then, vary not just in the characteristics ascribed to them, but also in the evaluation of those characteristics.

However, not only does the evaluation of a quality, say of inferiority or of aggression, differ from one stereotyped group to another, the evaluation for any given group can change from one situation to another. McGarvey devised an experiment to demonstrate this point. At a summer camp in the United States 30 Americans were tested on their attitudes to Japanese-Americans. They were informed that they would then be allowed to attend a show at the local theatre, but the show was cancelled at the last minute and instead they were given some complicated tasks to do. Following these tasks the subjects were given another attitude test and were now found to be less favourably inclined towards Japanese-Americans. Nothing had changed except some of the contextual features: the frame of reference. Translated to a contemporary British context, we might infer from this experiment that the evaluation of an ethnic minority group by white British will vary according to aspects of the current situation, like the availability of housing or jobs.

If our evaluations of others are influenced by our frames of reference, then it is inaccurate to regard these evaluations as fixed and absolute, yet it is often the case that we do so think of them. Many of the generalizations that teachers make at school are not particularly helpful to their teaching, even though they may not be directly harmful, as they are bounded by a limited frame of reference. Two children can be similarly labelled 'lazy', 'dull', 'awkward', 'difficult', but the relative nature of these tags may elude the teacher, even when one child comes from a disadvantaged home and the other from a home that is saturated with all the apparent advantages of a white middle class family.

Because of the situational characteristics of stereotyping, a person does not typically have *an* attitude to, say, Pakistanis. He will have many different attitudes depending on the circumstances. It also means that a general attitude regarding West Indians, for example, need not determine attitudes to individual West Indians. In other words, if a teacher has a general stereotype of West Indians and feels hostility towards them, this does not mean that he will necessarily feel unfavourably inclined to teach individual children of West Indian origin. A specific attitude to living next door to a member of a particular ethnic group may differ from the attitude, or predisposition, a teacher has to teaching a child from that ethnic group. The emotional overtones associated with a stereotype may shift from one moment to another and from one situation to another.

There are, then, two basic components of a stereotype:

A descriptive component
An evaluative component

A stereotype is a simple, rigid description of a person or group. That group is evaluated and the evaluation is often situation- or event-specific.

When a stereotypic description is attached to a racial, ethnic or national group, there is often an implication that the characteristics are genetically determined and so cannot be changed.

6.3 Some arguments against stereotyping

Several arguments are developed in the literature against the process of stereotyping:

Categorizing people is unacceptable.
Stereotyping is based on inaccurate data.
Stereotyping implies that the categories of people are based on inborn, unchangeable characteristics.
There is an implicit assumption that one's own cultural group represents the norm by which other groups should be judged.
Categorizing people becomes a self-fulfilling prophecy.
Stereotyping is often objectionable to individuals who are stereotyped.

One of the lines of argument against the use of stereotypes is simply that they are based on the categorization of people: that large groups of people—the working class, West Indians, policemen—are referred to as if they were composed of identical units, thus ignoring the individual differences that differentiate each of us. To accept this criticism is to imply that we ought to think not of groups, but rather regard each person and every event as unique. This is just not possible.

Take a noisy classroom situation. In some respects each classroom disturbance is novel (in the strict sense of the word), but if a teacher were forced to ignore the similarities between one classroom situation and another, then his task would be impossible. He would be unable to say 'Stop talking', or clap his hands, or use any of the other customary cues which children immediately recognize, on more than one occasion. Also, if the teacher is compelled to regard each disruption as a unique event, then he will be unable to make any predictions to guide his future responses. Similarly with children: if we are forced to abandon our categories for children—the child with learning difficulties, the urban child, the immigrant child—then we cannot plan in advance to meet the common needs of the children within these groups.

To form accurate anticipations is an obvious necessity for survival in all walks of life and we are all continually forming such anticipations which are based on our capacities for categorization. We make assumptions that a particular group will display similar characteristics or needs. For example, we may assume that immigrants from Pakistan will have common language problems; that emotionally deprived pupils will require a warm, supportive environment; and we make preparations on the bases of these assumptions. The critical requirement for a teacher in these circumstances is for him to be prepared to change his intentions in the light of his new knowledge of specific children.

The accuracy of a stereotype is often called into question. Here the important issue is the degree of accuracy that is demanded. There is some evidence to support many common ethnic descriptions, for example, but if there is just one exception does this invalidate our category? If not, then it becomes very difficult to establish a criterion for demonstrating its truth or falsity. Some would argue, for instance, that there is evidence to support the stereotype of West Indians as fun-loving and warm, and of Sikhs as aggressive and status conscious. But there will be cases where the descriptions could appropriately be reversed; but to do so in a few cases would not, in my view, invalidate the usefulness of categorization in general.

Stereotypes are not, then, to be condemned simply because they are generalizations that have been proven false on some occasions, since, for much of the time, we don't know whether they are true or false.

The most powerful criticism of stereotyping is that there is a hidden assumption that most stereotypes are based on inborn characteristics which cannot be changed. This tacit assumption is probably strongest with respect to racial stereotypes, in which the hidden assumption is that 'our' characteristics form the norm from which we judge all other groups, and the closer a group is to us in physical attributes the greater our affinity with it in most respects and the more favourable is any stereotype we hold for it. Yet there is no scientifically acceptable evidence to sustain the idea of genetically pure groups of people that are as large as complete 'races' of people.

An example of the effect of ethnocentrism associated with racial stereotyping can be found in the work of Katz and Braly in the United States. They found that Chinese were described as 'superstitious' and Italians as 'religious'. In both cases the descriptions say that a particular national group subscribes to a set of beliefs about the supernatural, but one group which displays the beliefs is called 'religious' by reference to norms with which most Britishers would not quarrel; while the other is described as 'superstitious' since the outward manifestation of its beliefs is unfamiliar to us, and contradicts our norms for this kind of behaviour.

A common description in ethnic stereotyping is the term 'dirty', when applied to groups other than our own. This is not just a description, it is also an evaluation: it says something about what ought to be. It not only labels an alleged difference between *us* and *them*, it also implies that our level of hygiene is the appropriate one, that anyone who does not bath as often as my group and me is inferior to us. But a little thought will indicate that it is not possible to establish an absolute standard for this. Cleanliness can only be judged by what is regarded as appropriate, and so it depends upon one's frame of reference.

The tacit assumption that whatever attributes we ascribe to other ethnic groups are not only unfavourable, but also innate, presents a very pessimistic perspective for the teacher if he were to be persuaded into accepting the validity of the common racial stereotypes. If we accept the fallacy that some ethnic groups are irremediably superstitious, dirty, of limited intelligence, fun-loving and so on, the job of teaching them could legitimately be reduced to conditioning and rote learning.

The assumption that racial characteristics, even if they are accurate descriptions, are innate rather than culturally induced, is generally regarded as having no scientific validity. To argue, for instance, that Negroes have a lower innate intelligence than white Americans, as Arthur Jensen has done, is to ignore the limitations of the instruments used to test intelligence. It also, and perhaps more importantly, ignores the issue of the purity of the sample of so-called Negroes. The tendency is to regard anyone with any recognizably Negroid physical features as 'Negro', no matter how diluted the splash of coloured blood. Any known Negro ancestry, however outweighed by white, tends to result in a person being categorized as 'Negro'. In America, after three centuries of mixed 'marriages', studies by Herskowitz (1930) and Stern (1954) indicated that 75 per cent of American Negroes have at least one white forbear and some 15 per cent have a predominantly white ancestry. So, allowing for a perfect instrument for measuring 'intelligence', we still cannot say that the differences in IQ prove that blacks are intellectually inferior to whites.

Table 6.1

To be stereotyped is often objectionable	So it is intolerable in a multicultural society
Racial stereotypes are based on the premise of inborn attributes	This assumption is inaccurate and can, when linked with the next criticism, be very damaging to the subject
A racial stereotype can become a self-fulfilling prophecy	
One's own cultural group is frequently used as the standard for judging others	We should try to understand the argument that most, if not all, values are culturally relative
People are categorized	This is a necessary part of dealing with a complex world; but categories should not be held inviolably, i.e., our descriptions should be open to change and we should release individuals from our personal categories as we get to know them individually

Another damaging feature of negative stereotyping is that the subject of the stereotype can come to believe that the description that has been given to him is true. It becomes a self-fulfilling prophecy. Because blacks are regarded by some writers as duller than whites, black people are in danger of believing it and their 'intelligence' can, over time, conform to that expectation. A term which is often used to conceptualize a related notion is 'stigma'. This is the idea that a person may suffer a distinguishing mark that sets him apart as inferior. If a particular community regards, say, green skin as a sign of inferiority, then a person with green skin cannot escape from the public submission that he falls short of what the community regards as normal and acceptable, and that he possesses all the unfavourable attributes that are associated with that skin colour.

The final argument against negative stereotyping cannot be countered, it is that many who are stereotyped find it objectionable, and so the process is alien to humane social relationships. Table 6.1 summarizes the arguments in order of salience.

6.4 Processes of stereotype acquisition

Staats and Staats (1958), investigating the acquisition of stereotypes, were able to demonstrate that stereotypes can be acquired through a form of verbal conditioning without the individual being aware of what is happening. In one of their experiments they told a group of subjects that they were going to be involved in an experiment on verbal learning. The words DUTCH, SWEDISH, FRENCH, ITALIAN, GERMAN and GREEK were presented visually 18 times, on flash cards. Immediately after this another group of words was presented aurally. The subjects were told to learn both lists, that is those they had seen and those they had heard. For one group the order of presentation was so arranged that the word DUTCH was always followed by unfavourable words from the aural list and SWEDISH was always followed by favourable words from that list. For a second group of subjects this arrangement was reversed. At the end of the presentation the subjects were given a booklet with a single word written at the top of each page and were asked whether that word had been seen or heard, or neither seen nor heard. They also had to rate the words on a 7-point scale, ranging from 'pleasant' at one end of the scale to 'unpleasant' at the other. On this scale, the first group of subjects rated DUTCH as 'unpleasant' and SWEDISH as 'very pleasant' and the second group of subjects reversed the ratings. So this experiment supported the view that stereotypes can be formed unwittingly and simply from the association of words without reference to any factual information.

Certain stereotypes are objectionable because they offend standards of accuracy and tolerance. They may also be offensive to those who are stereotyped. They may establish a self-fulfilling prophecy and stereotyping can stigmatize some people. Since stereotyping can be acquired through verbal conditioning, children's books should be scrutinized with care so that negative stereotypes can be identified and suitable action taken.

One of the most culpable perpetrators of unfavourable stereotypes in children's books is Enid Blyton. In 15 years of writing she is said to have produced some 300 books. In most of them she appears to have believed that if a statement is repeated often enough it acquires a patina of truth which can become a tilth for the cultivation of derogatory stereotypes. Some of the groups that are the subjects of over-generalization in her books are girls, policemen and 'the foreigner'; the simplistic picture she develops for each is found repetitiously in many of her books. Her ethnocentrism is blatant in many of her school stories, in which she makes a great deal of capital from a mythical English code of honour that is not possessed by any other nation. Foreigners are characterized as underhand, unclean, irrational and disloyal. To add to this catalogue of simplistic, rigid, over-generalizations, in an edition of the book called *The Three Golliwogs* published in 1968, the golliwogs are called Gollie, Woggie and Nigger. Part of the stereotype which is used to conserve her powers of description in the plots of several stories in this book is the assumption that all black people look alike.

Stories like those of Enid Blyton are not only unsavoury, and objectionable to black people, they may also help to create crude, distorted associations in the minds of young children which may be used in later life to justify the continuing exploitation of black people. During a child's formative years the negative stereotypes that are found in Enid Blyton's writing may be confirmed, supplemented and reinforced by other experiences in a racist country. For example, a pre-Christmas party for children of British soldiers in Germany was shown on television in 1980. At the party, attended by many white children and one black child, the 'good' children were rewarded by a white Santa Claus while the 'bad' children were chased by hideously dressed men with faces and hands coloured black. Most of the children screamed and yelled as one might expect, but the black child remained withdrawn, with a bemused look on her face.

6.5 Correcting stereotypes

Because of the social conflicts that can be generated by stereotyping and since its effects on human potential can be debilitating, a great deal of effort has been employed in trying to correct stereotypes, especially in America. Some of these efforts are reviewed here.

On the grounds that contact between the stereotyped and those who hold the stereotypes is enough to break down stereotypes and the prejudiced attitudes that may be associated with them, legislation in America now promotes multiethnic schools. This is compatible with the human relations model of education and is part of the rationale behind the formation of comprehensive schools, the bussing of pupils and invitations to representatives of stereotyped groups to school. There is some, though not unequivocal, evidence to suggest that as long as contact persists the attitudes may weaken and the stereotype is not used. However, once the person returns to a situation where the norms do not support tolerance, then the old habits of thought, speech and actions return. This raises the key issue in the field of attitude change: it is not so much whether change can be produced, but can it persist and does it generalize to other situations, in particular to those scenarios that supported the old stereotype?

Global approaches to attitude change have been challenged by the more specific methods suggested by Katz (1960). He argued that stereotypes, and in fact attitudes in general, serve several possible basic personality functions. If we are to be effective in changing them we must first identify the unwitting purpose a particular stereotype serves and then apply the techniques which are specific to that purpose.

Two of the functions described by Katz are ego-defence and value expression. When used as an ego-defence, stereotypes can prevent a person becoming aware of repressed conflicts that, if aroused, would create intense anxiety. Racial stereotypes may be an expression of latent hostility or latent sexuality, since many of the attributes ascribed to the stereotype are of a hostile or sexual nature. If this inference is accepted, it may be necessary for the person holding the stereotype to experience a catharsis, or cleansing, by being provided with support which enables him to talk out his problem with complete frankness.

Value expression is concerned with communicating one's values while at the same time maintaining consistency of identity. In such cases it may be necessary, according to Katz, to arouse the person by indicating inconsistencies and ambiguities in his beliefs so as to threaten his self-concept. For instance, the inconsistency of a person who subscribes to the Christian ethic while being a member of the National Front should be made evident to him and the greater consonance of an alternative set of attitudes might be discussed.

The ethics of attitude change need some consideration as the essential problem may be not whether we *can* change stereotypes, but whether we *should* as teachers engage in the process. At the root of the question are the concepts of power and coercion; the vulnerability of children and the compulsion attendant on their schooling. In short, should teachers try to manipulate children?

Both the Jesuits and Lenin are alleged to have said something like: 'Give me a child until he is eight years old and he will be a Jesuit (or a

Bolshevik) for life.' And Watson the behavioural psychologist said: 'Give me a dozen healthy infants, well-formed, and my own specified world to bring them up in and I'll guarantee to take any one at random and train him to become any type of specialist I might select—doctor, lawyer, artist, merchant-chief, and, yes, even into a beggar-man and thief, regardless of his talents, penchants, tendencies, abilities, vocations and race of his ancestors.'

The safeguard to manipulation of this kind in any 'normal' community is the range of influences and pressures to which children are exposed and which either cancel each other out, or present them with several alternatives from which to choose—just like selecting a washing powder. If a person is coerced into change he cannot be subjected to permanent coercion. This was the view of the judge in the Patty Hearst case in America in 1976: her brain might have been washed, but it could not have been in soak all the time she was held captive by the Symbionese Liberation Army.

The methods of stereotype correction that have been discussed here are the following:

> More education, on the grounds that truth dispels false beliefs.
> Contact between the stereotyped and those who harbour stereotypes.
> Identification of the function of the stereotype in each case and then the application of the specific technique that is indicated, e.g.:
>> if ego-defence, then talk through the problem so that an emotional cleansing is experienced;
>> if it is seen as an expression of a person's values, arouse dissonance in him by pointing out inconsistencies and ambiguities in his beliefs.

Some methods specific to the curriculum will be discussed in Chapter 7.

6.6 Stereotyping and teacher expectations

That teacher expectations can have a powerful effect in determining a child's performance at school has been discussed in Chapter 5, but a further consideration of the topic is relevant to the issues of the present chapter.

The study by Rosenthal and Jacobson (1968) drew the attention of teachers to the potent influence of expectation on pupil progress. While their study has been criticized, nevertheless it has been replicated elsewhere and experience suggests that there is some truth revealed in it. Briefly what they did was to take 18 classes and reported to the teachers that 20 per cent of the children were showing unusual potential for intellectual gains. Eight months later these 'unusual' children, who had been selected at random, showed significantly greater gains in IQ than the control group.

In their study Rosenthal and Jacobson had implanted an expectation in the minds of the teachers by reporting some inaccurate information as 'experts'. Stereotypes can create similar expectations.

Stereotypes can be created around many different focal attributes. Many of us, for instance, seem to stereotype first names. Particular names are associated with certain characteristics. At first thought we might dismiss this as mildly interesting but of no special significance to teachers. However, Harari and McDavid (1973) took some short essays written by children and gave each a pseudonym. Some of these pseudonyms were common, popular and attractive names, others were rare, unpopular and unattractive. The marks given to the essays were higher when they were linked with names which had a positive stereotype. The essays allegedly written by 'Lisa' always scored more marks than when they were allegedly written by 'Bertha'. 'David' and 'Michael' always scored higher than 'Elmer' and 'Hubert'. There is no evidence of the scores that would have been awarded to names from South Asia or the Caribbean, but it does suggest an interesting research project.

Dion et al. (1972) examined the effects of a physically attractive stereotype. They found that physically attractive people as a group were believed to have more desirable personalities, higher occupational status, to be more likely to have happy marriages, to be better parents and to enjoy more fulfilling lives. Dion did a similar study with adults with respect to their attitudes to the misdemeanours of children. It was found that a severe misdemeanour by an attractive child was much less likely to be assumed to be due to a permanent characteristic than was a misdemeanour by an unattractive child. Dion also found that two different sets of standards, and hence two different stereotypes, were operating in the cases of boys and girls.

Clifford and Walster (1973) also examined the effect of physical attractiveness on teacher expectations. They found that a child's attractiveness was significantly related to the teacher's expectations of the child's intelligence, to the parents' interest in education, to predictions about how far the child was likely to progress at school and to predictions about the child's popularity with his peers.

Crowl and MacGinities (1974) studied the influence of children's speech on teachers' expectations of the quality of oral answers. Tape-recordings of six white and six black 15-year-old boys speaking identically worded answers to typical school questions were played to 62 experienced white teachers. The teachers assigned higher grades to the answers when spoken by white boys than when they were spoken by black boys.

The evidence, then, that teachers' expectations are influenced by the stereotypes they have is varied and substantial, but what is more interesting and useful for the teacher is to have some idea of the processes that may be at work. One suggestion of the kind of mechanism that may be involved in transmitting the effects of teacher expectations to pupils has been described by Brophy and Good (1974).

An adaptation of the model described by Brophy and Good provides a plausible account of how racial stereotypes can influence expectations of the educational achievement and classroom behaviour of children from ethnic minority groups and thus the teacher's behaviour and, as a circular reaction, the actual achievement and behaviour of the pupils.

During the first days of the school year, or even before that, the teacher will consult his class list and record cards and will observe the interactions and overt characteristics of his pupils. The studies of Harari and McDavid (1973), Rosenthal and Jacobson (1968), Dion *et al.* (1972), and Clifford and Walster (1973) suggest that from some of the material gathered, such as name, colour, dress, hair style, physical attractiveness, IQ, style of handwriting, the teacher will create a mental impression, or stereotype, for at least some of the pupils. From these he will make predictions about the learning potential and future behaviour of his pupils.

In accordance with the differential expectations they will have formed, teachers begin to treat their pupils differently. The treatment will, to some extent, be determined at first not so much by the perceived needs of the children as by the expectations the teacher has previously formed. Since there will be a margin of error in the predictions, the appropriateness of the way in which the child is treated will vary.

Because of their different personalities and potentialities, and since the teacher will be treating them differently, the pupils will respond to the teacher in different ways. If a prediction is made that a boy, say, with a West Indian sounding name will be uninterested in school, the teacher may give the boy little attention and the lad may respond by becoming disinterested since any interest he does show will pass unrewarded. Again, a woman teacher may predict that a boy with the name of Singh will have scant respect for her as a woman, consequently she may treat him brusquely and thus cause the boy to be disrespectful to her.

Brophy and Good argue that, other things being equal, pupils will reciprocate the feelings and behaviour of the teacher. Each pupil will respond to the teacher with behaviour that complements and reinforces the teacher's particular expectations for him. Where the teacher holds inappropriate and rigid expectations, the pupil will become conditioned to respond with behaviour that approximates to, and therefore reinforces, the teacher's expectations. The longer the teacher continues to hold his expectations inflexibly for the pupil the more closely will that pupil's behaviour and achievement approximate those expectations. This will arise from a combination of the effects of the teacher's treatment of the child and the child's resultant opportunities and motivation to learn, his self-concepts and his general relationships with the teacher. That is to say, if a teacher holds a derogatory stereotype of a child from a minority ethnic group, he may give children of that group only a disproportionately limited amount of his time and attention; he may never smile at them, rarely touch them or establish eye contact, and be ungenerous in his comments about their efforts. Consequently, they will feel uncomfortable in the teacher's presence and disinclined to identify with his goals; the children's learning will be reduced and the teacher will be led to believe that his predictions are justified.

The differential treatment of pupils over the course of the school year will lead to disparities between different pupils in terms of process and product measures, such as attention, effort, self-concept, and measures of achievement. Where expectations are appropriate, or in those cases where the teacher responds rapidly to unexpected behaviours from the pupil, the teacher–pupil pattern of interaction will be largely predictable from knowledge of the pupil's general personality and classroom habits; and his achievements relative to those of his peers will be highly predictable on the basis of previous achievements.

When the stereotyped pupil enters the next class he carries with him into his relationship with the unknown teacher, who may or may not create a negative stereotype for him, the following debilitating consequences of his previous year at school:

Low achievement
An expectation of limited progress
An experience of an unrewarding relationship with a teacher

He carries with him an anticipation of failure.

The importance of this chapter for teachers can be summarized by returning to the task of defining 'stereotype'. In the light of the discussion it is clear that the essence of a stereotype is that it is a generalized category which is both descriptive and evaluative. So it is negative stereotyping rather than stereotyping in general that should be avoided because of its undesirable influences on classroom interactions.

Some specific techniques of recognition and avoidance will be discussed later in this text.

6.7 Summary

6.1 INTRODUCTION
An understanding of stereotyping is crucial since it makes an important contribution to our expectations for the children we teach.

6.2 WHAT IS A STEREOTYPE?
A stereotype is a simple, rigid description and evaluation of a person or group, the evaluation is often situation- or event-specific.

6.3 SOME ARGUMENTS AGAINST STEREOTYPING
To be stereotyped is often objectionable to those who are stereotyped.
Racial stereotypes are based on the premises of inborn attributes that cannot be changed.
A racial stereotype can become a self-fulfilling prophecy.
Ethnocentric standards are used to judge others.
People should not be categorized inflexibly.

6.4 PROCESSES OF STEREOTYPE FORMATION
Verbal conditioning, thus making books particularly influential.

6.5 CORRECTING STEREOTYPES
More education.
Contact between the stereotyped and those who form stereotypes.
Identify the function of the stereotype in the individual and apply the specific technique that may be indicated.

6.6 STEREOTYPING AND TEACHER EXPECTATIONS
Many features of children can create expectations in teachers which can become self-fulfilling:
Recorded IQ
Name
Physical attractiveness
Speech
Teachers' expectations condition the early interactions with their pupils, these influence achievement and behaviour.

7
Curriculum strategies to combat negative racial stereotyping

'How can we recognize negative racial stereotyping?'
'What curriculum strategies can we employ to combat negative stereotyping?'

7.1 Introduction

As we saw in Chapter 6, stereotyping can lead to prejudice and discrimination. Our understanding of the processes of stereotyping has illuminated the contribution of reading material to the development of prejudice and the role the school can play in reducing it. It is to this specific task that we now turn.

7.2 Reading and the development of stereotyping

Empirical research tends to confirm the assumption in the critical literature on children's books that the content of textbooks and literature for children influences attitude development in the reader. This is to say, books may achieve one of the major purposes for which they are written.

In a study which specifically examined the effects of books on children's attitudes, Trager and Yarrow (1952) divided a sample of six- and seven-year-old children into three groups. The first group was exposed to printed material emphasizing cultural pluralism; the second to printed material stressing cultural parochialism; and the third served as a control. The results showed that the first group accepted cultural variations as normal; the second group maintained or increased their attitudes of prejudice; and the attitudes of the third group remained unchanged.

A study by Fisher (1968) indicates that reading supported by discussion produces greater shifts in attitudes than reading alone. Other studies into the effects of reading on attitude change suggest that the greater a person's reading ability the wider the range of reading matter by which he is influenced. Indeed, Fehl (1966) argued that in an open society 'the widely read student will tend to form his opinions from a variety of sources while a student who reads little will be most influenced by textbook content, the latter being the major source of information to which he is exposed during school years'.

It is less than 10 years since books have come under extensive scrutiny in Britain for the racial stereotypes they convey. But many recent studies have revealed an alarming racial bias in many examples of popular children's fiction. (See Children's Rights Workshop, 1975; Dixon, 1977; Proctor, 1975; Stinton, 1979.) These studies of the treatment of racial minorities in children's books have uncovered a great deal of material which may adversely influence the attitudes of the child reader towards people of the ethnic minorities as well as being objectionable to the minorities themselves.

Most of the analyses of children's books have been intuitive, qualitative studies which reflect a literary perspective. But, despite the consensus that has slowly emerged on the criteria for these analyses, such as considerations of characterization, plot and tokenistic illustrations, the studies are essentially subjective in nature, they are non-cumulative and they are not amenable to statistical treatment. Neither are they helpful to the teacher or librarian who may need more objective criteria in selecting from among alternative titles when each of them contains some degree of bias. More recently in Canada and the United States techniques have been devised for quantifying bias in books and these tend to be more objective, more systematic and more accessible to generalization. It is not my intention to review a range of children's books or textbooks, but only to indicate some criteria and techniques that may be used in evaluating these books.

7.3 Qualitative techniques

Many authors of analyses of negative racial stereotyping in children's literature have used checklists in their work (see Stinton, 1979; Preiswerk, 1980). Others have adopted more intuitive approaches which may be no less effective in revealing racial bias, but may be difficult to replicate when adopted by the busy teacher.

A source common to many writers is *Interracial Books for Children*. This is the newsletter of the Council on Interracial Books for Children, Incorporated. Although it is written principally for an American readership it is also useful for British readers since it goes beyond a bare critique of specific books and gives analyses of current practices in the writing, editing, publishing and sale of books for teachers, parents and librarians. Whether or not they have used the guidelines published by the Council in 1974, many of the published analyses of children's books in Britain have used similar criteria and it is a modified version of these guidelines that I give below.

GUIDELINES FOR A QUALITATIVE ANALYSIS OF RACIAL STEREOTYPING

1. Check the illustrations for the following:
    (a) Stereotypes—are all non-whites portrayed as identical in appearance?
    (b) Tokenism—does it look as if the non-white figures have been coloured-in as an afterthought?
    (c) Roles—are whites dominant and non-whites shown against less affluent surroundings?
2. Check the plot for the following:
    (a) Standards for success—are they only those of the dominant group?
    (b) The skin colour of the characters who resolve problems.
3. Look for inaccuracies and inappropriateness in the descriptions of the life styles of minorities.
4. Note the sharing of power: is it largely in the hands of the dominant group?
5. To which ethnic group do the heroes and heroines belong?
6. What are the likely effects on a child of the ethnic portrayals in the book?
    (a) Will white children have feelings of superiority reinforced by what they read?
    (b) Are there worthwhile characters of their own group of whom minority group children can feel proud and with whom they can identify?
7. Do the author's cultural biases strengthen or weaken his work in any way?
8. Watch for value-laden words.
9. Pay particular attention to each of these features if the book was first published before the mid-1970s.

Similar criteria can be used for the appraisal of textbooks and they can be supplemented by the following questions:

1. Are white rather than non-white discoveries and aspirations described?
2. Are white people featured predominantly, to the complete or partial detriment of non-whites?

3. Is geographical exploration regarded as entirely beneficial to the people who are 'discovered'?

4. Are black independence and present-day development discussed?

5. Are struggles for freedom perceived as rebellion and are those who fight for freedom regarded as traitors and murderers, rather than as patriots?

6. Have facts about newly independent nations and the life styles of former colonial people been up-dated in new editions and reprints of books?

7. Are newly independent countries regarded as problematic for former imperial powers?

8. Is there an adequate portrayal of the social mix that exists in most countries today?

9. Are European values and life styles used as criteria for judging other ethnic groups?

10. Are technological advances used as the sole measure of progress?

11. Are typical personality traits ascribed to ethnic groups other than our own?

12. Are terms such as 'natives', 'hostile', 'huts', 'heathen', 'pagan', 'savage' and 'chief' used without elaboration or qualification?

13. In explaining national and cultural differences are concepts such as 'exploitation' and 'power distribution' used to castigate white men?

14. Are cultural differences regarded as biologically transmitted?

15. Is it assumed that the most fitted always survive and deserve any advantages that have accrued to them?

16. Are white Americans and Europeans described as developers of the rest of the world?

17. Are white Americans and Europeans regarded as doers and problem solvers and others given passive roles?

7.4 Quantifying negative racial stereotypes

Based on the premise that books play an influential role in the transmission of values from author to reader, the Carnegie Endowment for International Peace supported a content analysis of history textbooks in the years immediately following the First World War. Further studies until the start of the Second World War were also informed by the view that biased textbooks could influence international relations (Taft, 1925; Scott, 1926; Quillen, 1948). Then, in 1949, criteria for the analysis of history textbooks were provided by UNESCO in its *Handbook for the Improvement of Textbooks and Teaching Materials.*

More recently empirical techniques of content analysis have been developed in America and Canada as part of a search for greater objectivity and to permit statistical analyses of data. During the Second World War 'frequency analysis' was developed. This methodology assumed that if, for example, broadcasts in Germany showed increased use of such terms as 'patience', 'heroism' and 'sacrifice', then this indicated that the German authorities believed the war was going badly for them. Arising out of a study of the frequency of assertions made about ethnic minorities, Janis (1949) concluded that 'assertion analysis' was probably the most promising kind of content analysis for the study of their treatment in textbooks. Then, in the late 1960s Pratt (1969), in Canada, developed a form of assertion analysis called Evaluative Coefficient Analysis (ECO) based on the work of Osgood and his colleagues.

Evaluative Coefficient Analysis is based on the premise that the essence of evaluation is best found in the value judgements that are expressed, and the critical component in this respect is the favourability or unfavourability of the evaluative term. Pratt went on to list 293 common nouns and adjectives which account for approximately 88 per cent of the evaluative terms found in textbooks. These were categorized by groups of readers according to whether they reflected 'favourable', 'unfavourable' or 'neutral' evaluations. This list enables a text to be examined for the frequency of use of these evaluations and a score assigned to it based on the frequency count.

To illustrate the application of ECO Analysis let us take an extract from an essay on Southern Africa by Jan Morris. The paragraph reads:

> The country was founded and eponymously named, at the end of the 1880s, by the enigmatic British financier Cecil Rhodes, who supplanted its native chiefs by persuasion, force and skulduggery, hoping to find the country rich in gold. For thirty years it was administered, on behalf of the British Crown, by his British South Africa Company: an enormous commercial estate, 150,000 square miles of it, with not much gold after all, but priceless deposits of chrome and asbestos, and rich farming country where maize and tobacco thrive. When company rule ended in 1923, government passed not to the generally progressive British Colonial Office, which ran Kenya, Ghana, Nigeria and half a dozen other African colonies, but to a regime of local white settlers who imposed upon Rhodesia an inflexible structure of white supremacy.

Many of the evaluative terms used by Jan Morris in this passage are not included in the ECO list, but reference to that list provides either synonyms or a base from which individual judgements can be made.

Professor Pratt advises that one way of deciding whether or not a word is evaluative rather than purely descriptive is to apply the 'congruency test'. That is, to 'ask would the word be most appropriately applied to "saints" or "heroes", or alternatively to "sinners" or "villains"'. Doing this we find that the following evaluative assertions are made about Cecil Rhodes and white settlers:

Unfavourable evaluations:

>   supplanted, force, skulduggery, regime,
>   imposed, inflexible structure, supremacy

Favourable evaluations:

>   enigmatic, persuasion

The Coefficient of Evaluation is then calculated by applying the formula:

$$\frac{100 \times F}{F + U}$$

Where F = favourable terms and U = unfavourable terms. The coefficient for this passage is, then.

$$\frac{100 \times 2}{2 + 7} = \frac{200}{9} = 22.22$$

The higher the coefficient, up to a maximum of 100, the more favourable the passage to the group or individual concerned. The lower the coefficient, the less favourable the passage.

A copy of the ECO list of evaluative terms has been normalized on a sample of 250 middle-school children of 9 to 13 years of age and using conventional British spellings; this is provided in the Appendix.

7.5 Selecting methods of assessing stereotyping in books

A strong anti-empiricist bias among British educationists tends to resist the use of methods of quantifying stereotyping in children's books. However, methods of quantification do not exclude the use of qualitative approaches.

When quantification is undertaken analyses are carried out according to explicit previously formulated rules, thus removing a considerable element of subjectivity and randomness from the judgements that are made. The result is that systematization, objectivity and generalizability are increased.

One of the major criticisms of empirical approaches in any field of study of human behaviour is that emphasis on precision is often pursued to the neglect of significance, that is, statistical significance is achieved at the expense of problem significance. In addition, empirical techniques are frequently directed at the overt features of a communication while ignoring its latent aspects.

The view that is promoted here is that each has a part to play in raising the awareness of the reader, as well as in providing criteria for those who select books for children. Measurement has played a considerable part in educational research in contributing to our understanding of the learning/teaching process and Pool's (1959) assertion in relation to content analysis applies specifically as well as in a more general sense:

> It should not be assumed that qualitative methods are insightful and quantitative ones merely mechanical methods for checking hypotheses. The relationship is a circular one; each provides new insights on which the other can feed.

Since the unit of evaluation used in ECO Analysis is the assertions made about a nominated group of people, this cannot be regarded as an insignificant measure by any definition of that term. However, it is clear that no single method of analysis is capable of determining the treatment of ethnic minorities in books since bias can, in addition, be expressed through omissions, inaccuracies and distortions. Nevertheless, empirical methods, of which Pratt's ECO Analysis is a representative sample, may well provide a workable tool for use by teachers in addition to the more subjective approaches that are almost exclusively used at the present time. In addition they provide a criterion measure for teachers whose present book selection procedures are based on *ad hoc* decisions.

7.6 Curriculum strategies for combating negative stereotyping in reading material

One of the first systematic enquiries into the development in children of the idea of foreign countries and foreign people was undertaken by Piaget and Weil (1951). They concluded from a study of children of 5 to 10 years of age that concepts of foreign countries and people begin to form early in life and are aspects of children's moral development. Three stages were identified:

> Stage I, the egocentric stage—the world revolves around oneself.
> Stage II, the socio-centric stage—one's own group is the focus around which everyone and everything revolves.
> Stage III, the stage of reciprocity—this brings a realization that

'one's people are foreigners in other countries, foreigners are not foreign at home and that they too have feelings about belonging to their homeland'.

Since attitudes to other national groups form early in life and can be influenced by the material children read, one of the more contentious curriculum issues in this field is the question whether teachers should deny children access to books that transmit views of other people that are unacceptable to the teacher.

When the question of censorship is put in the case of books in general the response would appear to be largely in the negative since there seems to be a national aversion to censorship. However, it is often qualified when applied to specific groups of children. But because the dangers inherent in censorship and control may be no less than those that inhere in racial prejudice I take the view that it is a moral imperative to arm children to combat negative racial stereotyping, rather than to banish certain books since the power of censorship can be abused and one cannot be omnipresent. If we are effectively to prepare children to respond in a morally acceptable way to negative stereotyping in an educational context, children must be taught to recognize stereotyping when they meet it and then be disposed to engage in an exercise of personal judgement regarding the descriptions and evaluation of the groups and individuals concerned.

Techniques and strategies, other than the 'critical reading' implied above, can be deployed to help pupils to recognize and resist the persuasion to assimilate negative stereotypes and the prejudices that are associated with them. They are the following:

The provision of accurate information
Games and discussion
Teacher expectations
Teachers' responses to individual pupils
Modelling

Some of the techniques and strategies have been discussed in earlier chapters, those which have not will be discussed here.

CRITICAL READING
Critical reading has been described as the application of critical thinking to the reading process. It includes the following:

Questioning of and suspending judgement (*an Attitudinal Factor*).
Rational enquiry and problem solving (*a Functional Factor*).
Application of norms or generally accepted standards (*an Evaluative Factor*).

In a more detailed analysis, Robinson (1964) described 12 constituents of critical reading:

> Recognizing and discriminating between judgements, facts, opinions and inferences.
> Comprehension of implied ideas.
> Interpretation of figurative and other non-literal language.
> Detection of propaganda.
> Formation of and reaction to sensory images.
> Anticipation of outcomes.
> Generalization within the limits of acceptable evidence.
> Making logical judgements and drawing conclusions.
> Comparison and contrast of ideas.
> Perception of relationships of time, space, sequence, and cause and effect.
> Identification of the author's point of view or bias.
> Reaction to such literary forms as satire, irony and cynicism.

This concept of critical reading, in which the reader's function is not that of passively receiving the literal meaning of a passage, but one of actively working on the text, does not describe a finite skill or battery of skills, but rather a continuum along which each reader can progress.

An essential feature in translating some of the elements of critical reading into practice is discussion. Too often in the past teaching reading has been a low level activity in which children have been taught purely the recognition of words and with a consideration of only literal meaning. Both child and adult readers should be helped to develop the so-called higher order skills. With recognizing and responding to negative stereotyping as the aims, the following sequence can be employed:

1. Young children can be introduced to the idea of stereotyping through reading and discussion of familiar stories in which animals are stereotyped. *Red Riding Hood, Brer Rabbit, The Jungle Stories* and *Wind in the Willows* are traditional fare for children for a variety of reasons. They can additionally be used for teaching about stereotyping. The children can be asked to name the 'good' animals and the 'bad' animals. Or they can be asked to characterize, say, the fox, the rabbit, the wolf or the lion.

2. This can be followed by a discussion of the actual life of the animals in question, in which the facts are distinguished from anthropomorphized descriptions. The notion to be put across is

     that we cannot talk about bravery, love, slyness, cunning, in animals, since these are human qualities that we as human beings can only appreciate in others of our kind.

3. Similarities in the behaviour of all animals, including ourselves, can be considered in order to bring out the notion that all animals seek out food and shelter and appraise their environments to avoid harm and to satisfy needs.

4. The point that must then be emphasized is not the anthropomorphism but the selective descriptions that indicate stereotyping. The partiality of the description, for example, of foxes as only 'sly' and 'vicious' and the possibility of describing the way in which they care for their young.

5. The pupils can then be asked if they can recall stereotypes of human groups, starting with familiar examples, such as boys, girls, policemen, and the fallacies that exist in the biased selection of facts.

6. Pupils can then be asked to read, or be read to, say some of the Enid Blyton stories and be invited to describe some of the stereotyped characters, such as Mr Plod the policeman, the eccentric scientists and so on. Older pupils might be given some Westerns in which cowboys and native Americans are portrayed respectively as all good and all bad.

When pupils have been introduced to the idea of stereotyping and have been helped to spot examples in selected texts, they should be encouraged to identify stereotypes in more general reading and to discuss them with others.

PROVIDING ACCURATE INFORMATION TO COUNTERACT RACIAL
STEREOTYPES

The criteria identified earlier in the chapter can be applied to textbooks and other sources of factual information such as journals and magazines. As a rough and ready guide, one might look for the date of publication of the text, since a common concern for racial bias and stereotyping in books was not current until the 1970s, although there is no guarantee that books published since then are either factually more accurate or balanced in their presentations of national or ethnic groups.

Other clues to bias can be gained from a knowledge of an author's background and intentions as revealed by his nationality. Cultural allegiances and previous writing can also give a clue to a writer's biases.

The overriding question to ask is: Does the book make a positive contribution to the reader's development as a member of a multicultural society?

GAMES AND DISCUSSION

Games have a long history in education and can serve the achievement of a variety of objectives. The games described in the present context are recommended as vehicles which capture and sustain the interests of pupils and provide shared experiences which can generate discussion.

There are many sources of suitable games that can be used to focus pupils' attention on stereotyping and the essential ideas in them are common currency. Some sources of games that are relevant to the present objectives are to be found in the following references: Volkmor *et al.* (1977), Tiedt and Tiedt (1979), Baldwin and Wells (1980) and Hicks (1981). Here are two games that can lead to discussion:

1. Two blank cards, say 5 cm × 2.5 cm, are distributed to each pupil. Each pupil is then asked to write a word or phrase which describes himself. The labels are then offered to other pupils who may accept or reject them depending on whether they feel the label is a reasonable description of themselves. Every pupil must accept a label before one minute elapses. Pupils with the same or similar label group together for a discussion, which is introduced by the following questions:

Do you deserve this label?

Which other labels offered to you did you refuse?

Are there other 'labels' that could apply to you?

Which other labels would you have liked to have accepted?

The purpose of this game is to encourage insights into the partial nature of labels and how easy it is for them to stick.

2. Cards bearing the name of a country are distributed, one to each pupil. Each pupil keeps the name of his country secret and takes a turn of standing before the class to be questioned about the life styles and customs of that country. In this form of 'Twenty Questions' the pupil being quizzed may answer only 'Yes' or 'No', and the other pupils try to guess the name of the country from his response.

After playing the game a discussion can follow in which the principal question to be considered could be: How far did we rely on stereotypes to guess the countries?

DISCUSSION

The following starting points are suggested for discussion:

1. Ask what makes pupils alike as a group, e.g., a liking for the same music, sports, dress. Which characteristics cause comment from adults?

117

How do people come to be regarded as different?

What characteristics are highly regarded in our society?

Do some groups possess more of these characteristics and others less? Why is this so?

Are some characteristics of more worth than others in all circumstances?

2. Would you be indignant if you overhead people of other nationalities describing British people as 'untrustworthy', 'with no sense of humour', 'cold'?

What stereotypes are used to describe other people, e.g., Spanish, French, Italians, Americans, Australians?

Do they give a one-sided view of these people?

What do you think of the character Manuel on the TV programme *Fawlty Towers*?

What do you make of the fact that Manuel is shown as an Italian when the programme is shown in Spain, and Spanish when the programme is shown in Italy?

3. Which country would you most like to know more about? Why? If you met someone from a country you have heard others being critical of, would you automatically feel the same way? Why?

4. Describe a friend with a different skin colour from your own. Would a stereotyped description say anything about that person's favourable qualities?

7.7 Summary

7.1 INTRODUCTION

Reading material can contribute to stereotyping by pupils.

7.2 READING AND THE DEVELOPMENT OF STEREOTYPES

Reading followed by discussion produces greater shifts in attitudes than reading alone.

7.3 QUALITATIVE TECHNIQUES FOR IDENTIFYING RACIAL STEREOTYPES

7.4 QUANTIFICATION TECHNIQUES

Evaluative Coefficient Analysis (ECO)

7.5 SELECTING ASSESSMENT METHODS

Qualitative and quantitative techniques are complementary.

7.6 CURRICULUM STRATEGIES

8
Exploring cultural diversity in the classroom

'How can I encourage my pupils to take an interest in human differences?'

8.1 Introduction

Differences in people's appearances and in their ways of life should not be judged good or bad, but be accepted as normal examples of the diversity that is present in human beings. When we judge, say, differences in hygiene between a small nomadic tribe or Tibetan villagers and our own toilet arrangements, we tend to view them from a very partial perspective. We ignore the fact that we live cheek by jowl among peripatetic strangers, drink water that they have already drunk and breathe air that they have already breathed. When we pronounce on meals we have eaten in which the meat was underdone or overdone, too highly flavoured or too lightly flavoured, we are responding with palates that have developed preferences because of what we have become accustomed to eating. Since our intention is to promote cultural reciprocity we should develop in ourselves and encourage in our pupils the view that judgements of worth are inappropriate in such cases.

It is frequently the case in teaching that tips that can be used in the next lesson, or the one after, are eagerly sought by teachers. But when these ephemeral innovations are made without reference to a theoretical base, or in the absence of empirical evidence, they are no more than cosmetic activities designed to impress the short-term visitor and provide 'busy work' for the pupils.

For these reasons this chapter is written in two parts. First to provide some coherence to the exploration of human diversity, some aims and and objectives will be considered. Then some activities will be described to illustrate how aims and objectives may be achieved. Questions of the relevance of the activities to particular age ranges of child may arise. Experience leads to the opinion that most activities of the kinds described here can be quickly adapted for use with children at virtually any age level as long as the language used is appropriate, the pupils have not encountered the activities previously and account is taken of the ability levels of the pupils.

119

8.2 Guidelines for selecting curriculum content to stimulate an awareness of cultural diversity

One of the problems when establishing a multicultural bias to the curriculum is that old habits die hard. Here are some guidelines that will help to overcome the restrictions of familiar ways of curriculum planning.

1. When topics of national or global significance are considered the perspectives of other national or ethnic groups should be examined.
2. Accurate and up-to-date information should be supplied about the ways of life of other people.
3. Negative stereotypes should always be avoided. This is frequently achieved by referring to individual representatives of ethnic groups, although this carries with it the risk of distortion through the presentation of a notable, rather than a typical, example of the group.
4. The distortion attendant on illustrating differences between ethnic groups should be avoided by pointing to similarities across groups whenever possible.
5. Exploring cultural diversity—opening up choices for pupils of all ethnic groups and enhancing the self-esteem of minority group pupils—demands relevant curriculum content, teaching methods that encourage discussion and the modelling of appropriate behaviour.
6. Many of the activities in multicultural education can be used to exploit the experiences of individual pupils; in other areas of the curriculum, e.g., maths, science, a common base of shared experiences may be necessary.

8.3 Activities for exploring cultural diversity

SIMILARITIES AND DIFFERENCES

1. Pair off the children either randomly or in friendship pairs. Each pupil takes a turn to list or call out a similarity between himself and his partner. Then each child of the pairs in turn is required to list or call out a difference between himself and his partner. This can be played competitively between pairs.
2. Divide the class into two groups using simple criteria, e.g., boys/girls; those with birthdays from September to February/those with birthdays from March to August. Each

group will compete to draw up lists of similarities that are perceived within each group and lists of differences between the two groups.

3. The whole class draws up a list of characteristics common to the class and another list of differences between the class and other classes in school.

These three activities should lead in to a discussion of the ease with which people can be grouped and the advantages and disadvantages of grouping, as well as sensitizing pupils to human differences.

INDIVIDUAL DIFFERENCES

4. Illustrations can be cut from magazines to highlight individual differences in appearance. Illustrations of hair styles and clothes can also be collected and displayed.

These can be used to focus upon individual differences in discussion.

IDENTITY

5. Collect examples of ways in which people can be identified or draw up lists if examples cannot be gathered. These can consist of birth certificates, NHS numbers, numbers on the school roll, passport photographs, finger prints, foot prints, names—fore and surnames.

DERIVATIONS OF NAMES

6. There are a number of ways in which names can be explored: derivations; significance of certain names, e.g., the Scottish 'Mac', the Sikh 'Kaur' and 'Singh'. These are better investigated by the pupils interviewing people of the relevant ethnic group.

The pupils can also be asked to discover names that have equivalents in other languages, e.g., John (English), Ian (Scottish), Sion (Welsh), Shane (Irish).

CULTURALLY IMPORTANT CATEGORIES

7. Every culture develops a rich vocabulary around objects and concepts that are important to it. Pupils in groups should first select categories which seem to be important within a culture and then compile lists of words associated with each category. For example:

Bread—white, brown, granary, French stick

121

Clothes (Western)—shirt, blouse, trousers, jeans
Clothes (Asian)—shallwah, sarree, turban
Curry—madras, keema, vindaloo

With older pupils it would be worth while to base a discussion on how
language reveals our values; with suitable lists it would be possible to
make cross-cultural comparisons.

WHO IS IDEAL?

8. With the pupils in pairs, ask each pair to draw up a profile of the
   kind of person they would consider ideal. Where there is doubt,
   more than one profile might be compiled.

After, say, half an hour a discussion should reveal that there is no
universal ideal type, but rather that different situations make different
demands and so call for different strengths.

MUSICAL DIVERSITY

Pupils can be encouraged to listen and to move to music from different
ethnic groups. An increasing number of records of ethnic music is now
being released, below are some examples.

Caribbean (or with a Caribbean influence)
Catch a Fire—Bob Marley.
Green Valley—Militant Barry.
Street Level—Tribesman.
Forces of Victory—Linton Kwesi Johnson.
Tribute to the Martyrs—Steel Pulse.

African
An Anthology of African Music—UNESCO collection of 10 records.
African Sanctus—David Fanshawe (adaptations of African rhythms,
  with a book of that name).

Indian—classical
Music of India—Ragas and Talas—HMV ALP 1665.
Vilaejat Khan (Sitar)—HMV EALP 1266.
Folk songs and film music.
Shadi Kay Ghanay (Urdu wedding songs) CEMCPM 5113.
Iqbal Bachon Kay Liva (songs for children) CEMCP 5097.

Further reading
Beby, F. (1975) *African Music: A people's art*, Harrap.
Holroyde, P. (1972) *Indian Music*, George Allen & Unwin.
Roberts, J. S. (1973) *Black Music of Two Worlds*, Allen Lane.
Shankar, R. (1969) *My Music, My Life*, Jonathan Cape.

9
Exploring ethnic minority issues

'What does it feel like to be one of a minority ethnic group?'
'What are some of the problems of living in a society where one's own group is dominated by others?'

9.1 Introduction

Short though it is, this may be the most contentious chapter in this book. There is by no means general agreement that we should expose within the school curriculum the difficulties that the ethnic minorities experience. Some fail to perceive the problems of minority groups within our society; others may feel that if they are ignored for long enough solutions will emerge spontaneously: while others may honestly believe that to air grievances will only exacerbate them.

There is an alternative view, it is that to treat minority issues in the curriculum allows a heightened awareness to develop in white British children, while at the same time allowing opportunities for relatively cool reflection, under guidance, for both white British pupils alongside members of the current ethnic minorities.

In this chapter two topics are outlined and a short list of books that can be used for similar purposes. The first topic is a consideration of some of the contemporary problems of ethnic minorities in Britain; the second is a view of the genocide of native Americans in the last century. In both cases an outline is given of some of the crucial questions that may be discussed, with a limited indication of the kind of supporting material that may be used.

9.2 Topic: allocation of resources

The allocation of resources can be examined through unemployment levels, job levels, housing type and location, medical and nursing provision, and educational expenditure in relation to geographical location. In Tables 9.1–9.4 figures are given from Census reports and other sources.

Table 9.1 Job levels among races (figures in per cent)

Job levels	1966	1971	West Indians 1966	West Indians 1971	Pakistanis 1966	Pakistanis 1971	Indians 1966	Indians 1971
Non-manual	32	35	9	11	13	16	38	34
Skilled manual and foremen	35	34	40	41	20	21	25	27
Semi-skilled manual	15	13	26	24	32	33	20	21
Unskilled manual	8	8	22	16	31	23	12	11

(From: *The Role of Immigrants in the Labour Market*, Dept. of Employment)

Table 9.2 Percentage of shift work

	Professional/ managerial	White collar	Skilled manual	Semi-skilled manual	Unskilled manual
Whites	3	12	15	40	12
Minorities	11	7	29	46	31

(From: Smith, D. *The Facts of Racial Disadvantage*)

Table 9.3 Earnings

Median gross weekly earnings	Professional/ managerial/ white collar	Skilled manual	Semi-skilled/ unskilled
White men	£52.40	£39.30	£36.30
Minority men	£40.50	£35.60	£36.30

(From: Smith, D. *The Facts of Racial Disadvantage*)

Table 9.4 Housing: tenure by class (figures in per cent)

	Non-manual	Skilled manual	Semi-skilled manual	Unskilled manual
Owner-occupiers				
General population	67	45	33	20
Asians	59	81	82	85
West Indians	35	59	53	39
Rented from Council				
General population	16	39	46	56
Asians	6	4	4	2
West Indians	27	21	24	31
Privately rented				
General population	17	16	21	24
Asians	34	15	13	11
West Indians	35	20	23	29

(From: CRC. *Urban Deprivation, Racial Inequality and Social Policy*)

LANGUAGE ACTIVITY

Adverse comments are sometimes made by indigenous people of the 'unnecessary' expenditure on special language classes for migrants. The purpose of the activity described here is to demonstrate the extreme disadvantage suffered by a person who is unable to use the common language.

Each pupil is given a large sheet of paper, say A4 size, and a felt-tipped pen. The whole class should sit to face the front of the room in such a way that they can prevent others from seeing what they draw on their papers. A demonstrator and four observers are selected from the class.

The demonstrator's task is first to give non-verbal directions for drawing the series of squares as illustrated in Fig. 9.1. When this has been mimed without words, the demonstrator turns his back on the class, instructs the pupils to turn over their sheets of paper and then gives verbal directions, without actions for drawing the squares in the second figure.

While the class draw what they believe are accurate interpretations of the two sets of instructions, the observers note the reactions of the participants.

The demonstrator is asked to direct the class as quickly and as accurately as possible, trying to convey the shape, orientation, proportion and position of the squares both individually and in relation to one another. When giving non-verbal instructions the demonstrator must not draw on paper or blackboard. While giving the verbal instructions the demonstrator stands with his back to the class and with hands at his sides.

Diagram 1

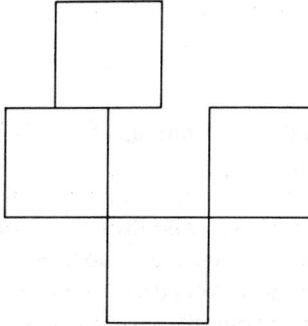

Diagram 2

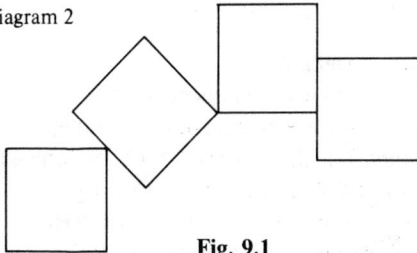

Fig. 9.1

When the tasks are completed the diagrams are shown and each pupil is awarded one point for each square drawn and further points for correct positioning of each square.

The observers comment on their observations of the process in terms of the hesitancy, misunderstanding, expressions of doubt and so on. The teacher concludes with comments on the accuracy and confidence with which such an activity is engaged in.

These shared experiences can be used in discussing the language problems of immigrants and the difficulties that are created when they are unable to share a common base of skills and abilities.

A set of profit and loss accounts can be drawn up of the costs and benefits of language education from the point of view of the minorities and their employers. For example, for the worker the balance sheet might read as in Table 9.5.

Table 9.5 Costs and benefits of language education

Benefits	Costs
Less frustration	Takes time and so less opportunity for
Better job prospects	overtime
More dignity	Takes effort and a risk of failure
Better pay	
More social opportunities	
More independence	

A book of newspaper and magazine cuttings can be kept of up-to-date information on the allocation of resources.

DISCUSSION

If there is not enough of a commodity for all to have unlimited amounts, how should it be shared?

With whom do you have most in common, a neighbour living in a similar house to your own, who dresses as you do, who talks with the same accent as you do; or a person who lives in a large isolated house set in beautiful gardens, whose children attend an expensive private school?

Would you change your answer if the first person had different skin colour from yours?

WHO ARE 'OUR OWN PEOPLE'?

If a person's language or lack of skills prevents him from getting a good job, does the country have a responsibility to help him?

Does everyone have a right to work? Are there any exceptions to this right, if the right exists? Are there any other rights in Britain?

Can we establish minimum living standards? How can we do this?

In what areas of life should minimum standards apply? Should the same standards apply to all groups, in Britain and in other countries?

What are the implications of minimum standards for those who are well above the minimum?

9.3 Topic: killing the native Americans

The purpose of this topic is first to give clues to the aspirations of the native Americans and of the white men; then to examine the Ghost Dance from the point of view of its escapist effect and to look for parallels at the present time.

> No white person or persons shall be permitted to settle upon or occupy any portion of the territory, or without the consent of the Indians to pass through the same.
>
> (Treaty of 1868)

> I have heard that you intend to settle us on a reservation near the mountains. I don't want to settle. I love to roam over the prairies. There I feel free and happy, but when we settle down we grow pale and die. I have laid aside my lance, bow and shield, and yet I feel safe in your presence. I have told you the truth. I have no little lies hid about me, but I don't know how it is with the commissioners. Are they as clear as I am? A long time ago this land belonged to our fathers; but when I go up to the river I see camps of soldiers on its banks. These soldiers cut down my timber; they kill my

buffalo; and when I see that, my heart feels like bursting. . . . Has the white man become a child that he should recklessly kill and not eat?

(Satanta, Chief of the Kiowas)

The Indian lands are the best in the State, and justice would demand, as well as every consideration of policy and humanity, that these fertile lands should be thrown open to settlement and the abode of civilized and industrious men.

(White agent of the Osaga Indians, in Kansas, 1864)

I am in favour of settling the wild lands into small parcels so that every poor man may have a home.

(Abraham Lincoln, 1 February 1861)

The Ghost Dance craze did not arise until Indian resistance had been broken; it was a gospel of despair. It was not a resistance movement, not even one advocating passive resistance, so much as a belief in miraculous deliverance from the white man and his depredations. Dead Indians would return to life and the buffalo in their myriads come back to the plains. A golden age for the red man would exist once more. The chief prophet of this belief was Wovoka, a Paiute in Nevada who had been brought up by Christians, and who proclaimed the second coming of a Messiah for early in 1891, in words that oddly jumbled Indian and Christian ideas together. . . .

The Ghost Dances went on all through the summer and autumn, embellishments being added, like the wearing of the ghost-shirt that was guaranteed to make an Indian impervious to the white man's bullets, until the agency whites became thoroughly though unjustifiably, alarmed, and began to fear another Indian outbreak. . . .

After a Ghost Dance lasting thirty hours, during which 'people went into trances by the dozen . . . several remained in trances as long as twelve hours. . . . People were so excited they trembled all over, their eyes rolled and the muscles of their faces twitched' . . .

The Ghost Dance cult was fundamentally harmless, perhaps indeed a good way of working off the frustrations of the by then almost helpless Indian tribes, if only the white man had not remembered Custer too vividly and discerned a scalp hunter inside every ghost shirt.

(The Ghost Dance)

DISCUSSION

What is the significance of calling the original inhabitants of the USA 'native Americans' rather than Red Indians? What is the stereotype of a native American that we have accepted in 'Westerns'?

The Treaty of 1868, like many other treaties, was broken by the white man. How do you feel these acts would have affected the native Americans?

How reasonable was it for Satanta, Chief of the Kiowas, to wish to stick to the traditional way of life?

As native Americans lived in only small groups with vast distances between them, was it reasonable for the white men to occupy the American continent?

Was it a good thing that the Ghost Dance allowed the native Americans to forget their troubles and made them look forward to a better life when they died?

What do we use at the present time to allow us to forget our troubles? Explore whether this is good or bad.

9.4 Books for young readers

Insights into the feelings of minorities can also be gained from recently written books. Here are some examples:

East End At Your Feet, Farrukh Dhondy, Macmillan, 1976.
Come to Mecca, Farrukh Dhondy, Fontaine, 1978.
To Be a Slave, Julius Lester, Puffin, 1973.
Long Journey Home, Julius Lester, Puffin, 1977.
Basketball Game, Julius Lester, Puffin, 1977.

10
Cases and situations in multicultural education

'What should I do if . . .?'

10.1 Introduction

This chapter has been designed to allow you to apply your understanding of the principles of multicultural education to specific case studies and familiar situations. It is based on the assumption that prior consideration will lead to the achievement of greater consistency between your actions in school and the values that guide them; greater consistency in this respect will lead to increased self-control.

If possible, try to discuss the problems posed here with a colleague and reflect on them in the light of your own experience, your reading and the values that you believe guide your professional actions.

10.2 'Should multicultural education be restricted to particular areas of the curriculum?'

Problem
In the staffroom of a multiethnic school a maths teacher, in the course of a discussion, stated that multicultural education should be restricted to Social Studies lessons. Is this point of view consistent with the principles of multicultural education?

Alternative responses

This point of view is totally acceptable since one of the particular intentions of Social Studies teaching which is not shared by other subjects is the development of pupils' understanding of social issues.

Since the total curriculum is concerned for the promotion of understanding and attitudes which lead to social competence within a tolerant society, this point of view is not acceptable.

It may be expedient to go along with this opinion in developing the curriculum since good race relations as an educational aim cannot be forced upon an unwilling staff.

Comment

This can be one of the most difficult types of problem to handle in both multiethnic and more homogeneous schools. The extent to which the view expressed by the maths teacher represents that of the rest of the staff is one of the important variables to be taken into account. If it is found in the majority of the staff it may well be that the restriction of education for good race relations to specific parts of the curriculum is all that can be aimed for with any hope for a measure of effectiveness.

Several questions must be posed in this situation. If a restricted view of multicultural education is adopted, should attempts be made to sensitize the staff in ways in which they might unwittingly offend children and their parents from the ethnic minorities? Again, is the maths teacher, and those who think as he does, to be made responsible for tasks which are fundamental to multicultural education, such as the vetting of textbooks and other materials in their own subject for evidence of racial stereotyping, or for lack of recognition of cultural diversity?

It should be remembered that, since multicultural education is predominantly concerned for the modification of attitudes and influencing behaviour, the most effective ways of achieving these aims are through an approach based on the whole curriculum.

10.3 'How can I cope with bullying that is associated with colour prejudice?'

Problem

A quiet, 12-year-old boy from a Pakistani family arrives in your classroom one morning looking very upset. He eventually tells you that he was 'beaten up' by four English boys. What action would you take?

Alternative responses

Talk to the boy in a kindly manner and advise him to keep away from the 'bullies' in the future.
Try to explain to him the nature of racial prejudice.
You feel that the behaviour of the 'white' boys is so reprehensible that you refer them to higher authority within the school.
You console the badly treated boy and work towards building up good peer relations within the class.
Any other suggestions.

Comment

An ideal solution would result in the prevention of any further abuse of the Asian boy and the acknowledgement by the bullies of the unsavoury nature of their behaviour. In this case one would also trust there would be no after-effects, such as recriminations on the part of the bullies, nor any apprehensiveness on the part of the victim. But this is too much to expect since, if colour prejudice lies behind the behaviour of the bullies, it will not be eradicated by any one action of the teacher.

You might consider the following actions in trying to reach an acceptable outcome. Some advice should be given to the victim on how he might avoid getting into a similar situation in the future. In addition, you could explain, in as unemotional a manner as possible, the nature of prejudice, scapegoating and related concepts as simply as seems necessary, not just to the Asian boy, but to the whole class. This might help your pupils to develop an understanding of their own feelings, attitudes and behaviours. While good peer group relationships do not guarantee freedom from bullying, to create the right atmosphere for good inter-pupil relationships is always a desirable goal in class as, in general terms, a friendly atmosphere will result in more effective learning.

Olweus (1978) proposed, in his study of 'bullies' and 'whipping boys', that the teacher should seek to build up good peer group relations. He cites the long-term effects of being a whipping boy from the study by Kagan and Moss (1962), in which they showed that, as adults, former whipping boys may be troubled by inner conflicts and anxiety in social situations. In this respect the study by Jelinek and Brittan (1975) of the friendship patterns of junior and secondary pupils may provide some guidance in resolving this issue. One of the striking findings of their research in ethnically mixed classes was the low level of inter-ethnic friendships. Considered in isolation, this might seem discouraging to those who seek greater integration, but the authors of this study sought the desired as well as the actual friendships. They found that at 8 years of age and at 10, 12 and 14 years, and for indigenous as well as for pupils of West Indian and Asian origins, all ethnic groups desired more friends from other ethnic groups than they actually had. Various barriers to inter-ethnic friendships were identified, these included: lack of facility in the English language; length of stay in England; cultural differences; the difficulty of changing established friendship patterns; lack of encouragement, or at worst, disapproval from society at large; discouragement resulting from the curriculum and visual environment of the school. Much other research on friendship patterns in general has also emphasized the importance of contiguity, that is of physical nearness in terms of location of homes and so on, and this, too, could be an important factor in the choice of friends from other ethnic groups. To

133

increase the possibility of cross-ethnic friendships may, then, require a many-sided approach which should involve other members of staff in a general collaborative effort throughout the school.

10.4 'How might a culture gap show up between myself and pupils from another ethnic group?'

Problem

Floyd, a boy of 11 years of age from a West Indian family, rarely makes a sound in class, yet he seems always exposed to his teacher's wrath; the teacher persistently reprimands him for minor misdeeds. Whenever he talks to the boy the latter never looks directly at him and this apparent rudeness only provokes the teacher to further rage. Over the last term Floyd's work has been getting increasingly behind that of the rest of his class. What action should the teacher take to remedy the 'behaviour problem' and increase his learning?

Alternative responses

The teacher should be much firmer with the boy, giving him a clear idea of the kind of behaviour and the level of work he expects from him. He should be punished if his misbehaviour continues.

The teacher should aim to become more tolerant of the child's apparent misbehaviour. To achieve this he should learn more about the kinds of behaviour that are regarded as normal in the boy's home culture.

Since the teacher is clear that the boy's behaviour is affecting his educational progress, he should refer him to the School Psychological Service for the possibility of formally recording his need for special educational treatment to be investigated. When his misbehaviour does not interfere with the smooth running of the class the teacher should try to ignore it.

Any other suggestions?

Comment

Each of the suggested responses carries with it the possibility of a counter-response from the child; rather than be precipitate in his actions the teacher should consider each possibility with care before committing himself to an action that might carry with it the possibility of a side-effect that could be more serious than the original difficulty.

There is an obvious culture gap between Floyd and his teacher who is apparently unaware that the boy's behaviour may be regarded as a sign of politeness in the culture from which he comes, where a child is expected to avert his eyes when reprimanded by an adult. In this case both the boy and his teacher have an ethnocentric and dissimilar view of what should be regarded as appropriate behaviour, consequently both are acting in ways that are compatible with the view of their own ethnic group, but each is incompatible with the other.

To be firmer with the boy will simply confirm in him what is probably a growing belief that the teacher does not like him, or, if he is more sophisticated, that the teacher is discriminatory and racist. Ignoring the child, too, may be interpreted as having a racist foundation.

Driver (1979) discusses several habits of West Indian pupils that are frequently misinterpreted by the teacher. He describes such actions as clicking, pouting and plucking the lips; actions which express derogatory feelings and are often not interpreted as such by white teachers and pupils.

The tendency to refer to children in general and West Indian boys in particular for recording and special school placement for behaviour problems even more than for learning difficulties has been noted by many observers in the last 10 years or so, for example, Coard (1971), Redbridge CRC (1979), Tomlinson (1978, 1981) and Driver (1979). It is not doubted that the behaviour of these pupils can be difficult to manage, but many accusations levelled at teachers allege that the cause of the difficulties lies in the discriminatory way in which the pupils are treated. A circular reaction is often set up since the troublesome behaviour arises from a lack of understanding between the teacher and the pupil and can lead to a reduction in the time the teacher spends with the pupil, so that he learns less easily than he might otherwise have done. The boy begins to perceive the teacher's apparent disinterest as discriminatory when he notes that the teacher shows a positive interest in pupils with white skins. Consequently, his behaviour becomes even more difficult to control since he might eventually 'write off' both school and those who are associated with it. When this attitude has hardened into alienation, he will include all whites in this category of people from whom he wishes to become dissociated.

As a person charged with facilitating the learning of all his pupils, the teacher has a responsibility to understand the backgrounds from which his pupils come so that any misunderstandings that can arise from the gap between his culture and theirs are minimized. Greater understanding should then be wedded to enhanced tolerance and a readiness on the part of the teacher to accept many of the behaviour patterns to which the child has become accustomed, if he subscribes to the ideal of a multicultural society. Once a firm positive relationship has become established between the teacher and the child, in which the teacher's unconditional acceptance of the child's ethnicity is confirmed, he might then begin to introduce him to the norms of the dominant ethnic group, if this is acceptable to the child and to his parents.

10.5 'How should I deal with inaccurate information in textbooks?'

Problem

You have noticed some inaccurate information in a history textbook in use in your school. It deals with the period of the Indian Raj and presents a view of the Indian nation as inferior to the British in all respects. What action would you take?

Alternative responses

> Since you believe that education should be particularly concerned for accuracy and tolerance, the books should be destroyed.
> As you are opposed to censorship of all kinds, the books should remain in use, but the pupils should be taught to recognize the biases in them.
> You should take no action on the grounds that the books have been in use for several years without causing any problems.

Comment

That the teacher should take no action is not an acceptable response in the light of our criteria for multicultural education, as this would offend the twin tenets of accuracy and tolerance. The argument that, since there is no direct evidence that reading specific books has produced identifiable adverse responses from pupils, there is no need to take action against the textbooks in question, is not acceptable as the effects of influences such as are found in reading matter and other media of communication are, generally, cumulative and often difficult to assess.

The liberal view that children should be educated to discriminate for themselves is very persuasive on the grounds that, if education is in part about tolerance, pupils should be presented with as wide a range of opinions and attitudes as is consonant with their abilities and maturity. These opinions should provide pupils with a basis for making their own judgements about issues such as these. However, here it is errors of fact and major exclusions that are involved, so, on the grounds of inaccuracy alone the books should not be used. If the books are likely to sustain unfavourable stereotypes of people of Asian origin, or are likely to offend children from the minority groups, they should be withdrawn from use pending a decision from the headteacher regarding their destruction.

10.6 'Is the celebration of Christmas appropriate in a multicultural school?'

Problem
In common with most British schools your school celebrates Christmas with a carol service, to which parents are invited; parties with food and games are organized for all children. But should schools respond to traditional Christian festivals, in particular to Christmas, in multiethnic Britain?

Alternative responses

> Stress the festivities and ignore the religious significance: 'I'm dreaming of a white Christmas' supersedes 'O come all ye faithful'. Since most religions celebrate the winter solstice, you might celebrate the festival of Christmas by a multi-faith approach that emphasizes the ethical lessons of Christmas and dilutes the Christian worship.
> All children should be encouraged to cooperate either as participants or as observers in a traditional combination of Christian worship and festivities. At appropriate times of the year the key festivals of other religions should be celebrated.

Comment
To stress the Christmas jollifications at the expense of the religious significance would offend many parents and others as it could be interpreted as removing the essential significance of Christmas. A similar inference could also be drawn from a multi-faith approach to the festival since the essence of Christmas in a Christian society is the celebration of the birth of the founder of the Christian faith, rather than the particular seasonal connection. Many would also refute the contention that it is essentially a re-statement of an ethic that Christianity embraces in common with other religions.

Since multicultural education is based on a concept of cultural reciprocity, the third alternative in which pupils of all ethnic groups are encouraged, but not forced, to celebrate each other's festivals, would seem to be the response which is most compatible with this position. To implement this principle with conviction would inevitably involve cooperation with representatives of religions other than Christianity.

10.7 'Can traditional intelligence tests be used as valid measures of the potential of ethnic minority pupils?'

Problem

Since teacher expectations are positively related to pupil performance a measure of the potential of each pupil would be useful as an objective guide to making realistic demands on him as well as being a valuable diagnostic tool.

Alternative responses

Children should not be tested.

While tests and testing are not rejected in principle, most of the tests in use in Britain have been standardized on white British children and are unfair to children from the ethnic minorities and so testing should be avoided at the present time.

There are some valid and useful tests available at the present time, when there is a specific task to be performed these tests should be used.

Comments

The process of testing and grading children and comparing one with another is abhorrent to many teachers. This attitude rests upon some often unstated assumptions. First, that a child's worth is in some way bound up with examination results. Experience suggests that there may be little relationship between examination results and the contribution that a person makes to society in adulthood or to the fullness of the life he later leads. Another contributory factor is that test results are rarely if ever used by the class teacher. Third, a situation in which a child is aware that he is being tested can be a traumatic experience for him. Then there is the added difficulty that tests may be used with children for whom they were not originally intended.

If a child for whom English is a second language is making little progress at school, it is occasionally difficult to decide whether or not the problem is located in the language difference, or an intellectual deficit. A suitable culture-free or culture-fair test could, in this case, be a useful diagnostic tool.

Although there have been continuing demands for tests that are culture-free or culture-fair, it is difficult to conceive of test items that are culture-free, if only because test items are expressed in linguistic form which, by definition, will be embodied in a culture. However, a culture-fair test, in the sense of one that can be used with children in a multicultural context without conferring an advantage on one cultural group over another, would seem to be possible. The complexity of translating this wish into practice is fraught with difficulties. In a highly technical article Petersen and Novick (1976) evaluated some half dozen models and variants on which culture-fair selection might be based. Each of these models is based on a different definition of culture-fair, and from these may be inferred distinctly different sets of values, psychometric models and solutions.

Within each definition, culture-fairness may reside in the selection of test items, in the calculation of different cut-off points for each ethnic group, or in a combination of the two. The emphasis adopted depends on the purpose for which the test is used. In the case of selection for special education, for example, the purpose may be to establish similar proportions of children from each ethnic group, to prevent the feelings of discrimination that may accompany disproportionate representation and the stigmatization that is still associated with special school or special class placement. In this case, while each child should be as familiar with the test content as any other child, the threshold criterion will be an ethnically related score on the test.

A recent development to accommodate the problems of the ethnocentric bias of traditional tests is the work based on learning ability. Although different cultures may interpret different behaviours as reflecting different levels of intelligence, the notion of learning ability or learning potential does not carry such connotations. The purposes of assessment according to this perspective are to differentiate between children whose present attainment is low because they have not had appropriate learning opportunities from those who have low attainment because they are innately slow learners. As Hegarty and Lucas (1978) describe, one of the advantages of such an approach to assessment is that the results guide the teacher to appropriate forms of intervention.

Epilogue

Multicultural education is a field filled with stumbling blocks and pitfalls for even the most cautious writer and teacher. Some are created by the limited agreement that exists on the use of some of the basic concepts, such as racism and discrimination. Others arise because ideologies differ on what should be the legitimate aims of education and the form of society to which we should aspire. Readers, too, may disagree on whether the principles of personal responsibility or inherited responsibility should govern our reactions to past exploitation.

In the introduction I discussed some of the essential values on which this book is based and the goals I have sought to achieve. If your values and educational goals coincide with those that motivated and guided me, I trust that reading this book has been a worthwhile activity. If you were unclear of the alternative value positions which might be considered, I hope that you are now more clear. If the values you hold are different from those represented here, you may have had cause to re-appraise them.

Whatever one's present position, with changes in society, there will always be a need to re-examine where we are heading in education; for this reason this book can only be a position statement rather than a definitive document.

Malcolm Saunders
July 1981

Appendix
Measuring stereotypes
Assertion analysis word list

The following words from the list compiled by Pratt (1972) were evaluated by 250 middle-school children (9 to 13 years). Many of the responses from this group departed from common usage and probably reflected an immature vocabulary. The words were also evaluated by 100 students of 18 + years and it is these evaluations that are given here. Where Pratt's evaluations, based on a Canadian sample, differ from the evaluations of the British sample, the former are given in parentheses.

able	+	butcher	—
achievement	+	calm	+
admirable	+	capable	+
advanced	+	careful	+
adventurous	+	charitable	+
afraid	—	charming	+
agile	+	cheap	—
alert	+	chivalrous	+
amazing	+	civilized	+
ambitious	+	clean	+
angry	—	clever	+
ardent	(0)+	cold	—
attractive	+	colourful	+
audacious	(0)—	common	(0)+
backward	—	complex	(0)+
bad	—	conscientious	+
barbarian	—	conspirator	—
beautiful	+	corrupt	—
bickering	—	courageous	+
bitter	—	courteous	+
blind	—	coward	—
blood-thirsty	—	crafty	(0)—
boastful	—	criminal	—
bold	(0)+	cruel	—
brave	+	cultured	+
bright	+	daring	+
brilliant	+	dauntless	+

dear	+	furious	—
dedicated	+	genius	+
delicate	+	gentle	+
delightful	+	gentleman	+
dependent	+	gifted	+
deserter	—	glorious	+
determined	+	good	+
devoted	+	goodwill	+
devout	+	gracious	+
dictator	—	grave	(0)—
dirty	—	great	+
disgruntled	—	greedy	—
dishonest	—	handsome	+
disloyal	—	happy	+
distinguished	+	hard	—
drunk	—	hardworking	+
eager	+	hardy	+
elegant	+	haughty	—
eloquent	+	healthy	+
enduring	+	heathen	—
energetic	+	helpful	+
enthusiastic	+	hero	+
experienced	+	honest	+
expert	+	honourable	+
extremist	—	horde	—
failure	—	horrible	—
fair	+	hospitable	+
faithful	+	hostile	—
false	—	howling	—
famous	+	humble	+
fat	—	idealistic	+
fearful	—	idle	—
fearless	+	ignorant	—
feeble	—	imaginative	+
ferocious	—	impatient	—
fierce	—	important	+
fiery	(0)—	independent	+
fine	+	industrious	+
foolish	—	inferior	—
foreign	(0)—	infidel	—
free	+	ingenious	+
friendly	+	insane	—

Word		Word	
insolent	—	pitiless	—
inspired	+	pleasant	+
inspiring	+	pleasurable	+
intelligent	+	plotting	—
interesting	+	plunderer	—
jealous	—	polite	+
just	+	poor	(0)—
kind	+	popular	+
late	—	primitive	—
lazy	—	problem	—
liar	—	promising	+
lively	+	proper	(0)+
lovely	+	proud	+
loving	+	prowling	—
loyal	+	pure	+
lurking	—	quality	+
magnificent	+	quarrelsome	—
martyr	(0)+	quick	+
massacre	—	quiet	+
mean	—	raiding	—
menacing	—	reasonable	+
merciless	—	rebel	(0)—
mistaken	(0)—	reckless	—
mob	—	remarkable	+
moderate	(0)+	renegade	—
modest	+	renowned	+
murderer	—	resentful	—
mutinous	—	resourceful	+
natural	+	respected	+
nice	+	respectful	+
noble	+	revengeful	—
normal	+	rich	(0)+
notable	+	right	+
outrage	—	rioter	—
outstanding	+	robber	—
pagan	—	sacrificial	(0)—
panic-stricken	—	sad	—
patient	+	savage	—
patriotic	+	scheming	—
peaceful	+	scholarly	+
pillager	—	selfish	—
pious	(0)+	sensitive	(+) 0

serious	(+) 0	treacherous	—
shrewd	(0) +	trickery	—
shrieking	—	troublesome	—
simple	(0) —	true	+
sincere	+	trustworthy	+
skilful	+	ugly	—
slaughter	—	uncivilized	—
slow	—	undisciplined	—
smelly	—	uneducated	—
soft	+	unfriendly	—
splendid	+	unreliable	—
strange	(0) —	unselfish	+
striking	+	unskilled	—
strong	+	untrustworthy	—
successful	+	useful	+
sullen	—	vain	—
superb	+	valiant	+
superior	+	valuable	+
suspicious	—	venerable	0
swarm	(—) 0	vicious	—
sweet	+	victorious	+
sympathetic	+	vigorous	+
talented	+	violent	—
tenacious	(0) +	warlike	—
terrible	—	warm	+
terrified	—	wasteful	—
terrifying	—	weak	—
terrorist	—	well-known	+
thief	—	wild	—
threatening	—	wise	+
thrifty	+	wonderful	+
tireless	+	worthy	+
tolerant	+	wrong	—
tough	(0) +	zealous	(0) +
traitor	—		

References

ALBERT, M. L. and OBLER, L. K. (1978) *The Bilingual Brain*, Academic Press.

BAGLEY, C. *et al.* (1979) *Personality, Self-esteem and Prejudice*, Saxon House.

BALDWIN, J. and WELLS, H. (1980) *Active Tutorial Work*, Books 1 to 4, Basil Blackwell.

BERGER, P. L. and LUCKMAN, T. (1966) *The Social Construction of Reality*, Penguin Books.

BOCK, G. (1976) 'The Jewish schooling of American Jews', unpublished PhD thesis, cited in H. J. Gans, 'Symbolic ethnicity', *Ethnic and Racial Studies*, **2**, 1, 1–20.

BRAH, A. (1978) 'South Asian teenagers in Southall', *New Community*, **vi**, 3, 197–206.

BROOKOVER, W. B., THOMAS, S. and PATTERSON, A. (1964) 'Self concept of ability and school achievement', *Sociology of Education*, **37**, 271–278.

BROPHY, J. E. and GOOD, T. L. (1974) *Teacher–Student Relationships*, Holt, Rinehart and Winston.

BROWN, D. M. (1979) *Mother Tongue to English*, Cambridge University Press.

BROWN, J. (1970) *The Un-melting Pot*, Eyre and Spottiswoode.

BROWN, R. and BELLUGI, U. (1964) *The Acquisition of Language*, University of Chicago Press.

BRUDIPRABHA, P. (1972) 'Error analysis', unpublished MA thesis, cited in J. C. Richards (1979), *Error Analysis*, Longman.

BULLOCK REPORT (1975) See Department of Education and Science.

BURNS, R. B. (1976) 'Self and teaching approaches', *Durham Research Review*, **36**, 1079–1085.

BURNS, R. B. (1979) *The Self Concept*, Longman.

CARROLL, J. B. (1955) *The Study of Language*, Cambridge University Press.

CHAPMAN, L. (1980) 'An experiment into monther-tongue teaching', *Trends in Education*, Spring 1980, 7–10.

CHILDREN'S RIGHTS WORKSHOP (1975) *Racist and Sexist Images in Children's Books*, Writers and Readers Cooperative.

CHRISTIAN, C. C. (1976) 'Sociological and psychological implications of bilingual literacy', in A. Simões, ed., *The Bilingual Child*, Academic Press.

CITY OF BRADFORD METROPOLITAN DISTRICT COUNCIL (1979) *District Trends, 1979*, Bradford MDC.

CITY OF BRADFORD METROPOLITAN DISTRICT COUNCIL (1981) *District Trends, 1981*, Bradford MDC.

CLARK, K. (1969) *Civilisation*, BBC and John Murray.

CLIFFORD, M. M. and WALSTER, E. (1973) 'The effect of physical attractiveness on teacher expectation', *Sociology of Education*, **46**, 248–258.

COARD, B. (1971) *How the West Indian Child is Made Educationally Subnormal in the British School System*, New Beacon Books.

COHEN, A. D. (1975) *A Sociolinguistic Approach to Bilingual Education*, Newbury House.

COMMUNITY RELATIONS COMMISSION (1977) *Urban Deprivation, Racial Inequality and Social Policy*, HMSO.

COOLEY, C. H. (1902) *Human Nature and the Social Order*, Scribners.

CORDER, S. P. (1974) 'The significance of learners' errors', in J. C. Richards, ed., *Error Analysis*, Longman.

CROWL, T. K. and MACGINITIES, W. H. (1974) 'The influence of student speech characteristics on teachers' evaluations of oral answers', *Journal of Educational Psychology*, **66**, 3, 304–308.

DEPARTMENT OF EDUCATION AND SCIENCE (1975) *A Language for Life* (The Bullock Report), HMSO.

DEPARTMENT OF EDUCATION AND SCIENCE (1981) *West Indian Children in Our Schools* (Interim report of the Rampton Committee), HMSO.

DEPARTMENT OF EDUCATION AND SCIENCE and THE WELSH OFFICE (1981) *The School Curriculum*, HMSO.

DILLAR, K. (1974) '"Compound" and "coordinate" bilingualism', *Word*, **26**, 254–261.

DION, K., BERSCHEID, E. and WALSTER, E. (1972) 'What is beautiful is good', *Journal of Personality and Social Psychology*, **24**, 3, 285–290.

DIXON, B. (1977) *Catching Them Young*, vol. 1, *Sex, Race and Class in Children's Fiction*, Pluto Press.

DRIVER, G. (1979) 'Classroom stress and school achievement', in V. S. Khan, ed., *Minority Families in Britain*, Macmillan.

DULAY, H. and BURT, M. (1974) 'Errors and strategies in child second language acquisition', *TESOL Quarterly*, **8**, 2, 129–136.

EDWARDS, V. K. (1979) *The West Indian Language Issue in British Schools*, Routledge and Kegan Paul.

ENLOE, C. (1980) *Ethnic Soldiers*, Penguin Books.

ERIKSON, E. H. (1968) *Identity, Youth and Crisis*, Norton.

ERVIN, S. M. and OSGOOD, C. E. (1954) 'Second language learning and bilingualism', *Journal of Abnormal and Social Psychology Supplement*, **49**, 139–146.

ERVIN-TRIPP (1972) Cited in J. Holmes (1978), 'Sociolinguistic competence in the classroom'.

FEHL, L. S. (1966) 'The influence of reading on the concepts and attitudes and behavior of 10th, 11th and 12th grade students', unpublished PhD thesis.

FISHER, F. L. (1968) 'Influence of reading and discussion on the attitudes of fifth graders towards American Indians', *Journal of Educational Research*, **62**, 130–134.

FISHMAN, J. A., ed. (1971) *Advances in the Sociology of Language*, vol. 1, Mouton.

FISHMAN, J. A. (1976) *Bilingual Education*, Newbury House.

FONER, N. (1975) 'The meaning of education to Jamaicans at home and in London', *New Community*, **4**, 2, 195–202.

GANS, H. J. (1979) 'Symbolic ethnicity', *Ethnic and Racial Studies*, **2**, 1, 1–20.

GARVIE, E. (1974) *Language for the Foundations of Reading and Mathematics*, Mimeo, City of Bradford.

GARVIE, E. (1976) *Breakthrough to Fluency*, Basil Blackwell.

GEISER, R. L. (1969) 'Some of our worst students teach', *Catholic Schools Journal*, June 1969, 18–20.

GEORGE, H. V. (1972) *Common Errors in Language Learning*, Rowley.

GHUMAN, P. A. S. (1975) *The Cultural Context of Thinking*, NFER.

GOODLAD, S. (1979) *Learning By Teaching*, Community Service Volunteers.

GOODMAN, K. S. (1976) *Miscue Analysis*, ERIC Clearing House.

GORDON, M. M. (1964) *Assimilation in American Life*, Oxford University Press, NY.

HAMBLIN, D. H. (1978) *The Teacher and Pastoral Care*, Basil Blackwell.

HARARI, H. and MCDAVID, J. W. (1973) 'Name stereotypes and teachers' expectations', *Journal of Educational Psychology*, **65**, 2, 222–225.

HARTNETT, D. (1974) 'The relation of cognitive style and hemispheric preference to deductive and inductive second language learning', cited in M. L. Albert and L. K. Obler, *The Bilingual Brain*, Academic Press.

HEGARTY, S. and LUCAS, D. (1978) *Able to Learn?* NFER.

HERSKOWITZ, M. J. (1930) *The Anthropometry of the American Negro*, Columbia University Press.

HERTZLER, J. (1965) *A Sociology of Language*, Random House.

HICKS, D. W. (1981) *Minorities: A teacher's resource book for the multiethnic curriculum*, Heinemann.

HILL, D. (1976) *Teaching in Multiracial Schools*, Methuen.

HIRO, D. (1971) *Black British White British*, Penguin.

HIRST, P. H. and PETERS, R. S. (1970) *The Logic of the Education*, Routledge and Kegan Paul.

HOLMES, J. (1978) 'Sociolinguistic competence in the classroom', in J. C. Richards, ed., *Understanding Second and Foreign Language Learning*, Newbury House.

JAMES, L. (1973) *Fiction for the Working Man, 1830–1850*, Penguin.

JAMES, W. (1890) *Principles of Psychology*, Holt.

JANIS, I. L. (1949) 'The problem of validating content analysis', in H. D. Lasswell *et al.*, *Language of Politics*, MIT Press.

JELINEK, M. M. and BRITTAN, E. M. (1975) 'Multiracial education, I', *Educational Research*, **18**, 2, 44–53.

JERSILD, A. T. (1955) *When Teachers Free Themselves*, Teachers' College, Columbia University.

KAGAN, J. and MOSS, H. (1962) *Birth to Maturity: A study in psychological development*, Wiley.

KAMINSKY, S. (1976) 'Bilingualism and learning to read', in A. Simões, ed., *The Bilingual Child*, Academic Press.

KATZ, D. (1960) 'The functional approach to the study of attitudes', summarized in C. A. Insko, *Theories of Attitude Change*, Appleton-Century-Crofts.

KATZ, D. and BRALY, K. W. (1933) 'Racial stereotypes of one hundred college students', *Journal of Abnormal Social Psychology*, **28**, 280–290.

KENNEDY, G. (1973) 'Conditions for language learning', in J. W. Oller and J. C. Richards, eds, *Focus on the Language Learner*, Newbury House.

KESSLER, C. (1972) 'Syntactic contrasts in child bilingualism', *Language Learning*, **22**, 221–233.

KHAN, V. S., ed. (1979) *Minority Families in Britain*, Macmillan.

KLAUS, D. J. (1973) 'Students as teaching resources', cited in S. Goodlad, *Learning by Teaching*, Community Service Volunteers.

KLAUS, D. J. (1975) 'Patterns of peer teaching', cited in S. Goodlad, *Learning by Teaching*, Community Service Volunteers.

KLINE, P. (1979) *Psychometrics and Psychology*, Academic Press.

KNIGHT, R. (1981) *Race Relations in Bradford*, Bradford Metropolitan District Council (mimeo).

LABOV, W. (1972) 'Some principles of linguistic methodology', *Language in Society*, **1**, 97–120.

LABOV, W. (1973) cited in J. Holmes (1978), 'Sociolinguistic competence in the classroom'.

LADO, R. (1957) *Linguistics Across Cultures*, University of Michigan Press.

LANCE, D. M. *et al.* (1969) 'A brief study of Spanish-English bilingualism', cited in A. D. Cohen (1975), *A Sociolinguistic Approach to Bilingual Education*, Newbury House.

LAWRENCE, D. (1971) 'The effects of counselling on retarded readers', *Educational Research*, 13, 119–124.

LAWRENCE, D. (1972) 'Counselling of retarded readers by non-professionals', *Educational Research*, 15, 48–51.

LEIN, cited in B. Cazden (1975) 'Problems for education', in M. Bloomfield and E. Haugen, eds, *Language as a Human Problem*, Lutterworth Press.

LIPPMANN, W. (1922) *Public Opinion*, Harcourt Brace.

LITTLE, A. (1975) 'Performance of children from ethnic minority backgrounds in primary schools', *Oxford Review of Education*, 1, 2, 117–135.

LOUDEN, D. (1978) 'Self-esteem and locus of control', *New Community*, VI, 3, 218–234.

MEAD, G. H. (1934) *Mind, Self and Society*, University of Chicago Press.

MIDWINTER, E. (1977) 'Teaching with the urban environment', in J. Raynor and E. Harris, eds, *Schooling in the City*, Ward Lock.

MUSGROVE, F. (1977) *Margins of the Mind*, Methuen.

NAGATA, J. A. (1974) 'What is a Malay? Situational selection of ethnic identity in a plural society', cited in C. Enloe (1980) *Ethnic Soldiers*, Penguin.

NEILL, A. S. (1960) *Summerhill*, Penguin.

NOVAK, M. (1976) *The Rise of the Unmeltable Ethnics*, Macmillan.

OLWEUS, D. (1978) *Aggression in the Schools*, Wiley.

OPIE, I. and OPIE, P. (1959) *The Lore and Language of Schoolchildren*, Oxford University Press.

PATTERSON, S. (1971) 'Immigrants and minority groups in British society', in S. Abbott, ed., *The Prevention of Racial Discrimination in Britain*, Oxford University Press.

PETERSEN, N. S. and NOVICK, M. R. (1976) 'An evaluation of some models for culture-fair selection', *Journal of Educational Measurement*, 13, 1.

PHILLIPS, S. U. (1972) 'Participant structures and communicative competence', cited by J. Holmes in J. C. Richards, ed., *Understanding Second and Foreign Language Learning*, Newbury House.

PIAGET, J. and WEIL, A. M. (1951) 'The development in children of the idea of homeland and relations with other countries', *International Social Science Bulletin*, III, 561–578.

149

PLATERA, D. (1973) 'Cultural pluralism', in M. D. Stent *et al.*, eds, *Cultural Pluralism in Education*, Appleton-Century-Crofts.

POOL, I de S., ed. (1959) *Trends in Content Analysis*, University of Illinois Press.

PRANDY, K. (1979) 'Ethnic discrimination in employment and housing', *Ethnic and Racial Studies*, **2**, 1, 66–80.

PRATT, D. (1969) 'An instrument for measuring evaluative assertions concerning minority groups and its application in an analysis of history textbooks approved for Ontario schools', unpublished PhD thesis, University of Toronto.

PRATT, D. (1972) *How to Find and Measure Bias in Textbooks*, Educational Technology Publications Inc.

PREISWERK, R. (1980) *The Slant of the Pen*, World Council of Churches.

PROCTOR, C. (1975) *Racist Textbooks*, National Union of Students Publications.

QUILLEN, I. J. (1948) *Textbook Improvement and International Understanding*, American Council on Education.

RAMPTON COMMITTEE, REPORT OF (1981) See Department of Education and Science.

REDBRIDGE COMMUNITY RELATIONS COMMISSION (1979) *Cause for Concern*. Redbridge CRC.

REES, O. A. and FITZPATRICK, F. (1981) *Mother Tongue and English Project*, vols 1 and 2, University of Bradford (mimeo).

RICHARDS, J., ed. (1974) *Error Analysis*, Longman.

RICHARDS, J., ed. (1980) *Understanding Second and Foreign Language Learning*, Newbury House.

RIEGEL, K. (1968) 'Some theoretical considerations of bilingual duplication', *Psychological Bulletin*, **70**, 647–670.

ROBINSON, H. M. (1964) 'Developing critical readers', in R. G. Stauffer, ed., *Dimensions of Critical Reading*, International Reading Association.

ROSEN, H. and BURGESS, T. (1980) *Language and Dialects of London School Children*, Ward Lock.

ROSENTHAL, R. and JACOBSON, L. (1968) *Pygmalion in the Classroom*, Holt, Rinehart and Winston.

SACHS and DEVIN (1976) cited in J. Holmes (1978), 'Sociolinguistic competence in the classroom'.

SAUNDERS, M. (1973) 'Home influences on ESN children', unpublished M.Phil. thesis, University of Nottingham.

SAUNDERS, M. (1977) 'A review of studies of the socio-familial backgrounds and educational facilities of the homes of moderately educationally subnormal children', *Child: care, health and development*, **3**, 407–423.

SAUNDERS, M. (1979) *Class Control and Behaviour Problems*, McGraw-Hill.

SAUNDERS, M. (1980a) 'The school curriculum for ethnic minority pupils: a contribution to a debate', *International Review of Education*, **XXVI**, 1, 31–48.

SAUNDERS, M. (1980b) 'Towards a curriculum for ethnic minority pupils', *New Community*, **VIII**, 1–2, 76–83.

SCHOOLS COUNCIL (1968–1973) *English for Immigrant Children* (SCOPE), Longman.

SCHOOLS COUNCIL (1971) *Religious Education in Secondary Schools*, Evans/Methuen.

SCHOOLS COUNCIL (1972) *Teaching English to West Indian Children* (CONCEPT 7–9), Longman.

SCOTT, J. F. (1926) *The Menace of Nationalism in Education*, Allen and Unwin.

SECCORD, P. F., BACKMAN, C. W. and SLAVITT, D. R. (1976) *Understanding Social Life*, McGraw-Hill.

SELINKER, L. (1972) 'Interlanguage', *International Review of Applied Linguistics*, **10**, 209–231.

STAATS, A. W. and STAATS, C. K. (1958) 'Attitudes established by classical conditioning', *Journal of Abnormal Social Psychology*, **57**, 37–40.

STERN, C. (1954) 'The biology of the Negro', *Scientific American*, **191**, 81–85.

STINTON, J., ed. (1979) *Racism and Sexism in Children's Books*, Writers and Readers Cooperative.

STONE, M. (1981) *The Education of the Black Child in Britain*, Fontana.

TAFT, D. R. (1925) 'History textbooks and international differences', *Progressive Education*, **II**, 92–96.

TARRANT, J. (1977) 'Teacher and pupil elicitations in small group discourse', Victoria University, Wellington.

TAYLOR, G. R. (1976) *A Salute to British Genius*, John Player Foundation.

THOMAS, E. (1980) *Wider Horizons*, City of Bradford MDC.

THOMPSON, M. (1974) 'The second generation—Punjabi or English?', *New Community*, **III**, 3.

THONIS, E. (1970) *Teaching Reading to Non-English Speakers*, Collier-Macmillan.

TIEDT, P. L. and TIEDT, I. M. (1979) *Multicultural Teaching*, Allyn and Bacon.

TOMLINSON, S. (1978) 'West Indian children and ESN schooling', *New Community*, **VI**, 3, 235–242.

TOMLINSON, S. (1981) *Educational Subnormality: A study in decision-making*. Routledge and Kegan Paul.

TOWNSEND, H. E. R. (1971) *Immigrant Pupils in England*, NFER.

TOWNSEND, H. E. R. and BRITTAN, E. M. (1972) *Organization in Multiracial Schools*, NFER.

TRAGER, H. G. and YARROW, M. R. (1952) *They Learn What They Live*, Harper.

TREMAINE (1974) Cited in M. L. Albert and L. K. Obler (1978), *The Bilingual Brain*, Academic Press.

VOLKMOR, C. B., PASANELLA, A. L. and RATHS, L. E. (1977) *Values in the Classroom*, Charles E. Merrill.

VERMA, G. and BAGLEY, C., eds (1975) *Race and Education Across Cultures*, Heinemann.

WALLER, P. and GAA, J. (1974) 'Motivation in the classroom', in R. H. Coop and K. White, eds, *Psychological Concepts in the Classroom*, Harper and Row.

WARD, G. W. S. (1977) *Deciding What to Teach*, National Association for Multiracial Education.

WARNOCK, M. (1977) *Schools of Thought*, Faber and Faber.

WEINBERG, M. (1977) 'A historical framework for multicultural education', in D. E. Cross *et al.*, eds, *Teaching in a Multicultural Society*, The Free Press of Glencoe.

WEINREICH, P. (1979a) 'Cross-ethnic identification and self-rejection in a black adolescent', in G. K. Verma and C. Bagley, eds, *Race, Education and Identity*, Macmillan.

WEINREICH, P. (1979b) 'Ethnicity and adolescent conflicts', in V. S. Khan, ed., *Minority Families in Britain*, Macmillan.

WESKER, A. (1980) *Love Letters on Blue Paper*, Penguin.

WYLIE, R. (1961) *The Self Concept*, University of Nebraska Press.

YANCEY, W., ERICKSEN, E. and JULIANI, R. (1976) Emergent ethnicity, *American Sociology Review*, **41**, 391–403.

YOUNG, M. F. D. (1971) *Knowledge and Control*, Collier-Macmillan.

Index

INDEX

McDavid, J. W., 103, 104
Mead, G. H., 36, 75
Melting pot, 13, 15, 27
Midwinter, E., 24, 87
Miller, T., 3
Minorities, ethnic, 3, 5
Modelling, 84–85
Motivation, 54
Multiculturalism, 13, 15, 16, 17, 18, 27
Musgrove, F., 78, 80
Music, 122

Nagata, J. A., 77
Neill, A. S., 11
Novak, M., 78
Novick, M. R., 139
Numeracy, 18

Obler, L. K., 32, 33, 43
Olweus, D., 138
Opie, I. and P., 69
Osgood, C. E., 31, 111

Patterson, S., 14
Peters, R. S., 11
Petersen, N. S., 139
Phillips, S. U., 60
Piaget, J., 1, 113
Platera, D., 12
Pool, I. de S., 113
Prandy, K., 22
Pratt, D., 111–112, 141
Preiswerk, R., 1, 108
Primitive, 3
Pringle, M. K., 11
Proctor, C., 108
Projects, 67–70, 71, 124–130

Quillen, I. J., 110

Racism, 1, 3, 22, 28, 88
Rampton Committee, 3
Reading (*see* Literacy)
Redbridge Community Relations Committee, 22, 135
Rees, O., 20, 23, 64
Relations, home-school, 37, 87
Resources, 20, 22, 124–128
Richards, J., 51
Riegel, K., 33

Robinson, H. M., 115
Rogers, C., 11
Rosen, H., 29
Rosenthal, R., 102, 104

Saunders, M., 50, 60, 87
Schema, 21
SCOPE, 17
Scott, J. F., 110
Seccord, B. F., 93
Self-concepts, 21, 36–38, 41, 43, 72–73, 80–82, 91–92, 105
  esteem, 24, 38, 75, 85, 86, 87, 91
  of teachers, 85
Self-fulfilling prophecy, 98, 99
Segregation, 12, 86
Selinker, L., 32, 43
Slavery, 3
Sociolinguistics, 59–62
Specificity, levels of, 5
Staats, A. W. and C. K., 99
Standard English, 34
Stereotypes, 75, 93–118
Stern, C., 98
Stigma, 99
Stinton, J., 108
Stone, M., 9, 20, 24

Taft, D. R., 110
Tarrant, J., 61
Taylor, G. R., 2
Thackray, J., 68
Theory, purpose of, 6, 7
Thompson, M., 14
Thonis, E., 62–63, 71
Tiedt, P. L. and I. M., 117
Tomlinson, S., 23, 135
Townsend, H. E. R., 14, 20, 54
Trager, H. G., 107
Tutoring, peer group, 66, 71, 82–85, 91

UNESCO, 111

Verma, G., 10
Vocational guidance, 22
Volkmor, C., 117

Waller, P., 85
Walster, E., 103, 104
Ward, G. W. S., 54, 55–56, 70